This item belongs to

Sarah Taylor

W9-BON-004

Writing for the Information Age

Other Norton books

by Bruce Ross-Larson

Edit Yourself

Stunning Sentences

Powerful Paragraphs

Riveting Reports

Effective Writing

Writing for the Information Age
Light, Layered, and Linked

Bruce Ross-Larson

W. W. Norton & Company
New York   London

Copyright © 2002 by Bruce Ross-Larson

All rights reserved
Printed in the United States of America
First Edition

For information about permission to reproduce selections from this book, write to
Permissions, W. W. Norton & Company, Inc., 500 Fifth Avenue, New York, NY 10110

The text of this book is composed in Univers
Composition by Communications Development Inc., Washington, D.C.
Manufactured by The Courier Companies, Inc.
Book design by Peter Grundy
Production manager: Andrew Marasia

Library of Congress Cataloging-in-Publication Data
Ross-Larson, Bruce Clifford, 1942–
    Writing for the information age : light, layered, and linked / Bruce Ross-Larson.
        p. cm. — (The effective writing series)
    Includes index.
    ISBN 0-393-04786-5
    1. English language—Rhetoric. 2. Technical writing—Computer network resources. 3.
Report writing—Computer network resources. 4. Online data processing. 5. Technical
writing. 6. Report writing. I. Title.

PE1408.R727 2002
808'.042'0285—dc21

                                                                    2001056260

W. W. Norton & Company, Inc., 500 Fifth Avenue, New York, N.Y. 10110
www.wwnorton.com

W. W. Norton & Company Ltd., Castle House, 75/76 Wells Street, London W1T 3QT

1 2 3 4 5 6 7 8 9 0

To Starling Lawrence

For his trust and patience

61060

400282

Acknowledgments

I thank my colleagues at the
American Writing Institute
for their help in testing,
indeed refining, the precepts
and techniques in this
book—Meta de
Coquereaumont, Alison
Strong, Paul Holtz, Steve
Kennedy, Wendy Guyette,
Molly Lohman, Fiona
Blackshaw, Kelli Ashley,
Susan Quinn, Stephanie
Rostron, Jessica Saval,
Garrett Cruce, Megan Klose,
and Walter Hemmens. I also
thank Peter Grundy for his
diagrams of the various
structures.

Author's note

Today's impatient readers pay attention mainly to writing that engages them—to writing that allows them to find quickly and easily what might be of interest.

With this in mind, I assemble here a hundred or so techniques for engaging your readers. I describe each technique in a sentence or two. I rely heavily on example—believing, as one sage said, that an ounce of example is worth a ton of abstraction. And where appropriate I inject a short comment.

As the guide on the next two pages shows, I cover each technique on two facing pages, with the left narrow panel presenting the technique, the two main panels the examples, and the right narrow panel a comment, along with occasional links to related material. My hope: that you find quickly what might be useful.

How to use this book

Title
Names the technique

Technique
Explains the technique
in two or three
sentences

Example
Gives examples of the
technique in use

❌ Not this
✅ But this

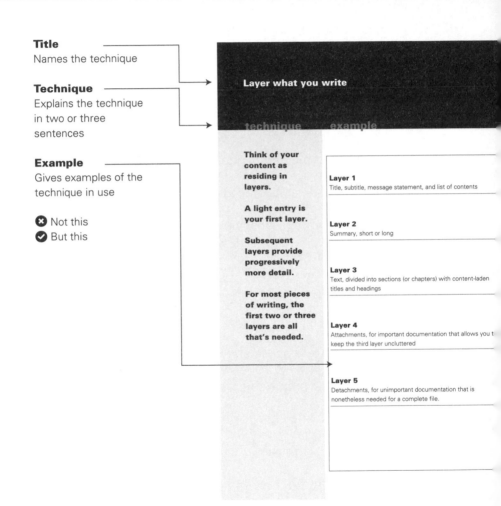

Layer what you write

technique   example

Think of your
content as
residing in
layers.

A light entry is
your first layer.

Subsequent
layers provide
progressively
more detail.

For most pieces
of writing, the
first two or three
layers are all
that's needed.

Layer 1
Title, subtitle, message statement, and list of contents

Layer 2
Summary, short or long

Layer 3
Text, divided into sections (or chapters) with content-laden
titles and headings

Layer 4
Attachments, for important documentation that allows you t
keep the third layer uncluttered

Layer 5
Detachments, for unimportant documentation that is
nonetheless needed for a complete file.

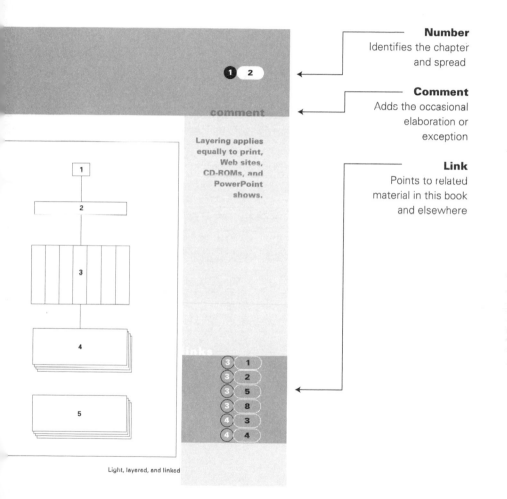

1 **2**

comment

Layering applies
equally to print,
Web sites,
CD-ROMs, and
PowerPoint
shows.

Number
Identifies the chapter
and spread

Comment
Adds the occasional
elaboration or
exception

Link
Points to related
material in this book
and elsewhere

1

2

3

4

5

links

3 1
3 2
3 5
3 8
4 3
4 4

Light, layered, and linked

Contents

The first precept of this book: keep your writing light, especially at the beginning, to engage your readers, not repel them. Second, slice your content into layers of progressive density and detail, so that your readers skip across the surface and go deeper only when they find what engages them. And third, where possible and useful, try to inject links that point your readers to related material that is easy to find. Those three precepts—light, layered, and linked—are essential when writing for the information age.

To lighten your writing is the easiest of the three—to have light entries into a piece of writing, to be light on the page and screen. To layer your content takes a sense of structure, moving from light opening to heavier pieces of argument and detail. And to link one piece of content to another takes a special effort, to point your readers to what is relevant without having the pointers get in the way. To do all three is to be kind to your readers—for a piece of writing, a Web site, a PowerPoint® show.

technique example

Keep the first things your readers see light and engaging.

Draw readers in with an engaging title— and possibly a subtitle.

Then tell them the main message, usually in your first sentence.

Also give them a list of contents that conveys the essence of your argument.

Title

❌ Libraries in the future

✅ Buildings, books, and bytes: Libraries and communities in the digital age

Message statement

✅ Library leaders want the library of the future to be a hybrid institution that contains both digital and book collections. The public loves libraries but is unclear about whether it wants libraries to reside at the center of the evolving digital revolution—or at the margins.

Communicative list of contents

Executive summary Views of library leaders and the public on the future of libraries in the digital age

1. Public visions, private reflections
2. Public support for libraries
3. Key public policies as the context for libraries
4. The prospects for a coordinated, collaborative effort

Appendix Public opinion survey on the future of libraries in the digital age

Make text easy on the eye

How library leaders see the future

Library leaders want the library of the future to be a hybrid institution that contains both digital and book collections. And they assume that it will be the librarian "navigator" who will guide library users to the most useful sources, unlocking the knowledge and information contained in the vast annals of the information superhighway.

Some library leaders envision a digital "library without walls" in which users gain access to almost unlimited amounts of information through home computers or at remote terminals located around the community. They also envision a time when one library's collection will, because of growing electronic capabilities, become everyone's collection.

Library leaders see a continuing role for the library building. As a central and valued community meeting space, the library will become more of a civic integrator and a locus of community information on health, education, government, and other local services.

Most pieces of writing begin, continue, and end with dense blocks of text, relentlessly repelling readers.

It helps to lighten text with short sentences, short paragraphs, and bulleted lists—and to use open line-spacing and narrow columns.

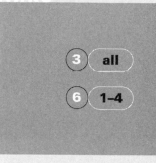

3 all

6 1–4

Light, layered, and linked

Layer what you write

Think of your content as residing in layers.

A light entry is your first layer.

Subsequent layers provide progressively more detail.

For most pieces of writing, the first two or three layers are all that's needed.

Layer 1
Title, subtitle, message statement, and list of contents

Layer 2
Summary, short or long

Layer 3
Text, divided into sections (or chapters) with content-laden titles and headings

Layer 4
Attachments, for important documentation that allows you to keep the third layer uncluttered

Layer 5
Detachments, for unimportant documentation that is nonetheless needed for a complete file

comment

Layering applies equally to print, Web sites, CD-ROMs, and PowerPoint® shows.

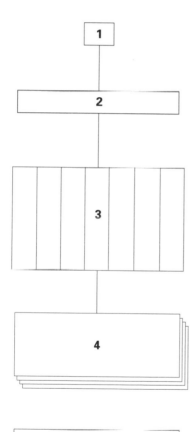

links

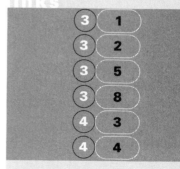

Light, layered, and linked

Link what you write

Readers appreciate explicit links to more detailed content and to related content.

The first step in linking is to point to greater detail within a piece—and next, outside the piece.

Communicative, detailed contents

❌ 2. Background

✅ 2. The world is changing and graduate education has not kept up

Targeted links

Each entry in a table of contents created by Microsoft® Word is a hyperlink to the corresponding text. Word's Document Map® feature also uses hyperlinks.

Informative cross-references

❌ . . . (section 3)

✅ . . . (for more on how this might work in practice, see page 27 in section 3)

Informative citations

❌ . . . (Porter 2001)

✅ . . . (for another view on the rebirth of corporate strategy, see Michael Porter's provocative *Strategy Is Back*, 2001)

Indexes

Graduate education 2–4, 8–11, 17–24, 31–37
    Changing numbers in specific fields 2
    Problems with current system 4, 32
    Signs of stress 4
    Programs increasing the numbers in specific fields 32–33

Contents with rollovers

The principles of layering and (internal) linking are built into the content menus of well-designed Web sites.

The key in linking is to allow your readers to know what is relevant and what irrelevant—so that they follow only the links to content of use to them.

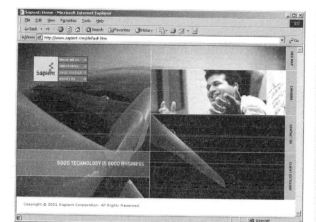

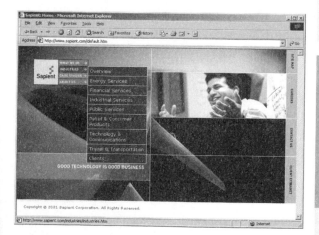

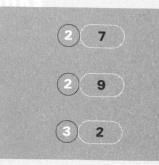

Good tools make jobs easier, and writing is no exception. But finding the right words for your thoughts is more daunting than choosing the right hammer or drill bit. Consider the *Oxford English Dictionary*—an immense tool chest—with 291,000 entries.

No thesaurus, spell checker, or prefabricated model will turn your first line into the start of a great piece of writing. But you can move beyond simply banging away at the keyboard, like the many writers in the O Spontaneous Me school of drafting.

How? By using some readily available tools to help you preserve order as you separate what you need to say from all the other things that you might say. These tools can also help you in layering and linking the content of what you write.

Online resources

Writing resources abound online. Dictionaries, style guides, grammars of languages living and dead. E-zines and discussion lists for writers, editors, and publishers. Reference works and search tools. And billions of bytes of great literature.

So vast are the resources that the tough question is not how to find them—it's how to organize them.

Convert your browser's Favorites or Bookmarks list into an effective filing system by creating a detailed folder structure that suits the way you work.

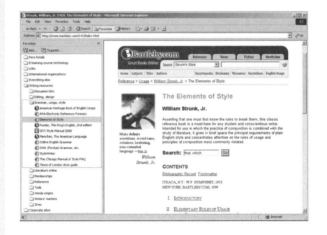

Dictionaries

Merriam-Webster's Collegiate Dictionary. The online version gives you everything the printed volume does, plus it will pronounce your word and link you to sites where it's used. www.m-w.com

yourDictionary.com. With 1,800 dictionaries in 250 languages, you can check the spelling of "supersede," but if you need a Breton or Chamorro grammar, they're there, too.
www.yourdictionary.com/index.shtml

Good writing

ClearWriter.com. An online system of tools, training, and resources that improves business and professional writing. www.clearwriter.com
ClearEdits.com. Searches your prose for problems and suggests solutions. www.clearedits.com
[Confession: The author of this book works for ClearWriter.]

Grammar and style

The Elements of Style. William Strunk's 1918 classic, pre–E. B. White. www.bartleby.com/141/index.html
Web Style Guide. The online version of Patrick Lynch and Sarah Horton's guide contains excellent advice on preparing text for the Web. info.med.yale.edu/caim/manual/contents.html/horsepub.com

Reference works and search tools

Britannica.com. Quick, encyclopedic access to articles, related maps, illustrations. Index feature gives you quick access to related content. Free, but the pop-ups swarm like gnats. www.britannica.com
Library of Congress online catalog. That's right, the entire catalog is online. Amazing depth and scope, plus great advice on effective searching. catalog.loc.gov

Organizing favorites can be cumbersome in Internet Explorer (the browser).

If you're organizing a big set of online resources, use Windows Explorer (the file and folder display) to create your folders and to arrange their contents.

links

www.plainlanguage.gov

www.clearwriter.com/resources.htm

technique   **example**

With online tools you can look up a word in a dozen dictionaries at once.

You can also configure text so that any word you click is looked up in the (multilingual) dictionary you specify.

And you can download specialized glossaries (or build your own) and get the full etymology of any word in the English language.

On your browser, look it up for free at M-W.com . . .

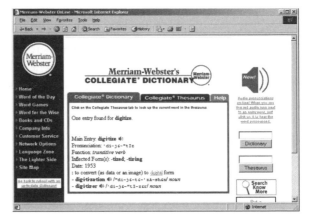

Or for a fee—with etymology and examples—at OED.com . . .

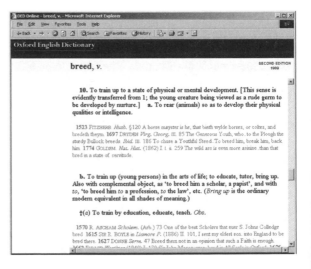

comment

Or in one of hundreds of glossaries at
Babylon.com.

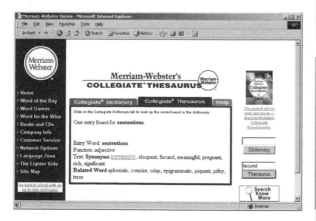

Find synonyms in the thesaurus at M-W.com.

**Uncritical use
of a thesaurus
can backfire
if you miss
nuances
between words.**

**When in doubt,
consult a source
that offers
examples of the
word in context.**

links

www.babylon.com
www.m-w.com
www.oed.com
www.onelook.com
www.wordweb.co.uk
www.worldwidewords.com
www.yourdictionary.com

Used with respect for their limitations, spell checkers and their grammar-checking cousins are valuable tools.

Although not substitutes for dictionaries and grammars, they are starting points for reviewing your writing.

You can configure your grammar checker to flag various types of problems (TOOLS > OPTIONS > SPELLING & GRAMMAR > SETTINGS).

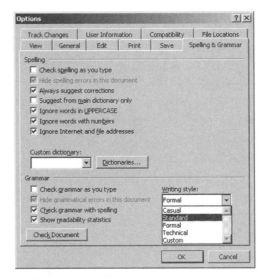

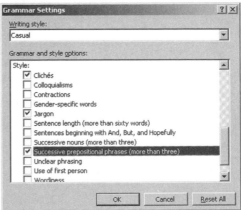

But spelling and grammar checkers can lead you astray.

It can be tiresome to spell-check bibliographies and reference lists because of the many names.

If you mark such text as exempt from review, remember to check titles carefully.

2 4

7 14

Style choices

To be consistent in spelling—and in using hyphens, capitals, initials, numbers, and punctuation— is nearly as important as avoiding typographical errors.

Keep track of your style choices in a four-column document. You can keep that document open as you draft, pulling it to the fore when you need to—and as your choices arise.

Numbers
one to nine
10 and above
2 percent
$15 million
1998–99
1999–2001
12- to 14-year-olds

Punctuation
Use the serial comma
    (light, layered, and
    linked)
No commas after short
    introductory phrases that
    do not contain verbs (By
    1989 the economy had
    collapsed)

Special terms
capacity building
federal funds rate

A
acknowledgment
anti-inflation
annexes
appendixes

B
benefited
box 3.1 (not Box 3.1)
breakup
buses

C
carryover
coauthor
coworker
cross-country

D
decision making
decision maker(s)

E
e-commerce
e-mail
European Union (noun)
EU (adj.)
euro
education sector

F
figure 5.1 (not Figure 5.1)
formulas
forums

G
the government of
GDP, GNP—spell out on
    first occurrence only

H
high-income couples
health sector
homegrown strategy

comment

I
indexes
interdepartmental
Internet
intraregional

J
judgment

K
kilowatt—kw when used
extensively in a docu-
ment (only when pre-
ceded by a numeral)

L
latter—don't use; repeat
the item or say "the
second" long-standing

M
macroeconomic
microeconomic
mid-1970s
modeled, -ing

N
neoclassical
newly established
nonexport
nongovernmental

O
occurring
occurred
offshore
online

P
periurban
President Bush
prime minister

R
risk taking (unit modifier
and noun)

S
second (not secondly)
sectoral

T
table 4.3 (not Table 4.3)
transaction costs
targeting
trade-off

U
U.S. (adj.)
United States (noun)

W
waterlogged
Web site

**For some
invariable
choices
(utilize → use,
utilization → use),
think about
plugging your
preferences into
the autocorrect
function of your
word processor
(TOOLS > AUTOCORRECT
> REPLACE).**

2 3
2 5
7 14

www.clearwriter.com/
resources.htm#styleguides

Tools

The autocorrect feature of your word processor can also make your writing more consistent and therefore easier to read.

Enter your choices for words that have more than one accepted spelling (*advisor* and *adviser*) and others that you often mispell— er, misspell.

Use your word processor's autocorrect feature to keep track of words with more than one accepted spelling.

Here are some candidates for invariable changes that you may want to add to your autocorrect library:

a lot of → many
achieve reductions → reduce
additional → more
alteration → change
and also → and
and/or → and
append → add
apprise → inform
component → part
concerning → about
conform with → conform to
data is → data are
despite the fact that → although
e.g. → for example
end product → product
end result → result
et al. → and others
etc. → and so on
firstly → first (and so on)
have an impact on → affect
heretofore → until now

i.e. → that is
in spite of → despite
in the event that → if
in view of the fact that → because
inasmuch as → because
included in → in
irregardless → regardless
large-sized → large
lengthy → long
located in → in
made a decision → decided
media is → media are
might possibly → might
moment in time → time
must necessarily → must
period of time → period
pertaining to → about
rapidity → speed
so as to → to
towards → toward
until such time as → until
utilization → use
utilize → use

comment

Be careful that your autocorrect entries don't backfire on you—say, by changing *advisory* to *advisery*.

links

Tools

technique · **example**

Use your word processor's find function to find words that signal opportunities to tighten your writing (EDIT > FIND).

Search for participles (verbs ending in *-ed*), passive voice (a passive verb followed by *by*), and such Latinate words as those ending in *-ion.*

Also search for conjunctions (*and, or, but*) that join phrases and clauses that often can be manipulated to good effect—or cut.

ClearEdits™, a plug-in for Microsoft® Word, searches your drafts for problems and suggests hundreds of helpful edits.

Compare: affect, effect.
effect (the verb: bring about)
affect (the verb: influence),
effect (the noun: result)

Try:
caused by,
because of

Many workers lack basic writing skills. This has a huge affect on business—U.S. businesses lose over $60 billion in productivity each year due to employees who do not write well. In order to make the lessons that are in our instructor-led courses [Cut?] available to writers everywhere, we developed ClearWriter. ClearWriter is a next-generation blended training solution for effective writing which includes online training, online tools, online mentoring, instructor-led workshops, and printed materials.

ClearWriter doubtlessly cuts the time writers spend [Cut?]

If you are defining a noun or pronoun, change 'which' to 'that'; if you are adding information about a noun or pronoun, put a comma before 'which.'

comment

Use your word processor to track the average number of words in your sentences and sentences in your paragraphs. The following screen shot reports on "readability statistics" for this section.

Readability Statistics		? X
Counts		
Words		2689
Characters		15390
Paragraphs		273
Sentences		148
Averages		
Sentences per Paragraph		2.2
Words per Sentence		13.6
Characters per Word		5.0
Readability		
Passive Sentences		4%
Flesch Reading Ease		55.9
Flesch-Kincaid Grade Level		8.7
		OK

TOOLS > OPTIONS > SPELLING & GRAMMAR >
READABILITY > STATISTICS

Combine frequent search and replace operations into a macro (or key sequence) that you can run with a single keystroke or from a button you create and place on the toolbar (TOOLS > MACRO).

links

7 1–4

7 14

www.clearedits.com

www.editorsoftware.com/
stylewriter

Tools

Format choices

technique

In reading as in life, people are usually uncomfortable when they don't know where they are or where they're going.

So, sprinkle your writing with signs: running headers and footers, introductory paragraphs, and bold page and section numbers.

These and other conventions increase your readers' comfort—and their power to absorb your message.

example

Arrange your writing on pages that are easy on the eye and offer plenty of navigational cues.

1 Catching up with the advanced countries

For a long part of history, China was the lar gest and most advanced economy in the world. Over the past 2,000 years China's share of global GDP hovered around 25% until the late 1700s. In 1820 China accounted for 33% of global GDP. Then from 1820 to 1950 it suffered great internal strife and foreign exploitation. Its GDP collapsed—as it increased elsewhere. As a result China's share of global GDP fell to just 5% in 1950 (figure 1.1). China's per capita income also led the Western Europe until about the 12th century and world until the 18th century (table 1.1). Then other parts of the world caught up and roared by.

Outside of China, the codification and exploitation of scientific and technical knowledge and the development of economic incentives and institutions were stimulating the creation and effective dissemination and use of knowledge.

What happened in China? It had developed some radical innovations—printing, gunpowder, shipping, calculus. But many of them more as curiosities or amusements, not for commercial exploitation.[1] In the 16th century, the age of sea exploration, China had larger and more technologically advanced ships

For a long part of history China was the largest and most advanced economy

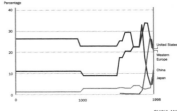

FIGURE 1.1
Share of world GDP by selected country or region, year 0–1998
Percentage

CHINA AND THE KNOWLEDGE ECONOMY

Create a document template to store character and paragraph formats ("styles") that you use frequently. Use the Organizer in FORMAT > STYLE menu to import styles from your template or from a pleasingly formatted document.

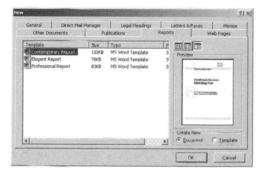

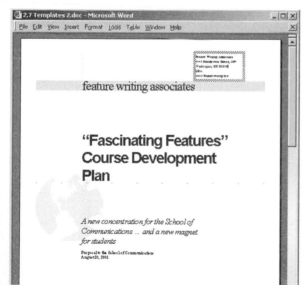

Write as if you are giving directions to a visitor.

Once you decide on your navigational conventions, keep them consistent and put them on a style sheet.

links

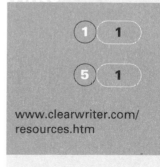

www.clearwriter.com/resources.htm

Tools

technique　　**example**

**To help
you think in
hierarchies and
identify your
main and
supporting
messages, use
a document
plan or model.**

**Review draft
structures using
Microsoft®
Word's Outline
view or
Document map
feature** (VIEW >
OUTLINE **or** VIEW >
DOCUMENT MAP)**.
Outline view
displays your
text in
hierarchical
form, allowing
you to drag or
click blocks of
text into new
locations in the
hierarchy.**

Some common document models:

Divisions Divide a subject into parts and subparts.
Sequences Of steps, milestones, events—wherever
there is a logical sequence.
Solutions Open with a statement of the problem,
move to detailing cause and effect, and finish with the
solution.
Groups Arrange disparate details (or findings or problems) in logical groups and subgroups.

Groups
Grouping allows you to arrange disparate details (or findings or problems) into logical
groups and subgroups. The process often reveals hidden connections.

Introduction of disparate details and how they can be grouped

¶ 1 _____

¶ 2 _____

Heading for group 1

¶ 1 _____

¶ 2 _____

Heading for group 2

¶ 1 _____

¶ 2 _____

Heading for group 3

¶ 1 _____

¶ 2 _____

Heading for group 4

¶ 1 _____

¶ 2 _____

Conclusion

¶ 1 _____

¶ 2 _____

Viewing your work in progress as an outline can help you think about its structure—and experiment with others.

```
Fascinating Features.doc - Microsoft Word                    _□X
File  Edit  View  Insert  Format  Tools  Table  Window  Help    X

  ◇  Choosing a topic and developing a theme
     ◇  Choose a topic
     ◇  Develop a working theme
     ◇  Reality check: Consider your limitations
     ◇  Refine your theme

  ◇  Collecting information
     ◇  The art of the interview
     ◇  Organize your notes and refine your theme
     ◇  Cherchez la femme (or l'homme)

  ◇  Outlining your story
     ◇  The flexible structure
     ◇  The inverted pyramid
     ◇  The chronology
     ◇  Alternating viewpoints
     ◇  Outline your story

  ◇  Writing your story
     ◇  The opening
     ◇  The significance cluster
     ◇  The caveat cluster
     ◇  The body
     ◇  Quoting people
     ◇  The ending
  ◇  Postscript: Edit yourself
```

When arranging text using new tools, always work with a copy; keep your original safe.

And don't confuse Word's Outline view with Outline numbering. The first is simplicity itself; the second, a Pandora's box, and no aid to good writing.

links

4 all

5 2

www.clearwriter.com/
tools.htm

Tools

technique   example

Mark your heads not just for style (appearance) but also for placement in an automatically generated table of contents (INSERT > REFERENCE > INDEX AND TABLES > TABLE OF CONTENTS).

That will save you the trouble of creating (and re-creating) the table of contents as you write and revise.

Mark headings so that you can later generate a hyperlinked table of contents.

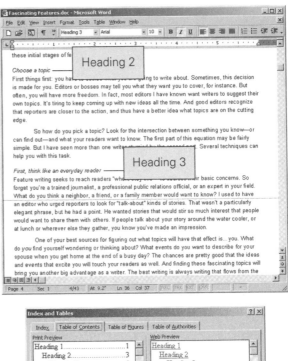

comment

Once you've marked the headings in your piece, you can easily regenerate the table of contents after revising your text.

It's a short step from marking your material for a table of contents to tagging it for use in a relational database.

Fascinating Features.doc - Microsoft Word

File Edit View Insert Format Tools Table Window Help

Caption ▾ Arial ▾ 10 ▾ **B** *I* U

Contents

Heading 1

Page 1   Sec 1   1/43   At 1"   Ln 1   Col 9   REC TRK EXT OVR

links

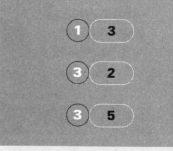

Tools

Information isn't the scarce commodity, as a leading economist wrote in the 1970s. Attention is. So, what can you do to sustain your reader's attention?

Several things. Start with a compelling title and list of contents, making your headings communicate the structure and messages of your line of argument. Next, give readers a light opening—to engage rather than repel them.

Then, think what you can do to keep things light on the page. Many of these suggestions are more visual than textual. Short paragraphs, rather than long, with line spaces between them, and other devices to break up what would otherwise be dense text—bullets and boxes, charts and tables, even pictures.

This may seem more the realm of design than writing, but writers today need to think of the visual if they want to sustain their readers' attention.

technique   **example**

The title of your piece of writing is the first thing your readers see.

If engaging, it will draw them in with a clear idea of your subject and perhaps even your messages.

Subtitles give substantive elaboration to an eye-catching title. Use them as a signal, not a crutch.

Buildings, books, and bytes
Libraries and communities
in the digital age

**Do African countries pay
more for their imports?**
Yes

A retiring nation
Italy has far more pensioners
than it can afford

The gift of fear
Survival signs that protect
us from violence

Many writers
start with a title
before they
write—and then
stay with it,
without trying
to refine it.

To arrive at an
engaging title,
try many as
you progress
with writing—
combining and
recombining
key words.

**2001 things to do
in a recession**
1. Get a parachute

Who knows
Safeguarding your privacy
in a networked world

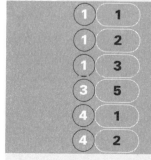

Attention-sustaining
devices

Communicative contents

Lists of contents should be much more than labels— they should reveal the architecture of what you're writing and communicate your messages and points.

Indeed, more than helping your readers find something, they should help them learn.

This, from *The Elements of Style:*

An Approach to Style

1. Place yourself in the background
2. Write in a way that comes naturally
3. Work from a suitable design
4. Write with nouns and verbs
5. Revise and rewrite
6. Do not overwrite
7. Do not overstate
8. Avoid the use of qualifiers
9. Do not affect a breezy manner
10. Use orthodox spelling
11. Do not explain too much
12. Do not construct awkward adverbs
13. Make sure the reader knows who is speaking
14. Avoid fancy words
15. Do not use dialect unless your ear is good
16. Be clear
17. Do not inject opinion
18. Use figures of speech sparingly
19. Do not take shortcuts at the cost of clarity
20. Avoid foreign languages
21. Prefer the standard to the offbeat

This, from *The Death of "e" and the Birth of the Real New Economy:*

The Rise of the Real New Economy
Technology Enables, Business Changes
The Business Technology Timeline
The Rise of the Real New Economy
 Stage 1. Brochureware
 Stage 2. E-Commerce
 Stage 3. E-Procurement
 Stage 4. Electronic Marketplaces
 Stage 5. The Digital Economy
Dynamic Business Ecosystems

Communicative contents often rely on imperative forms, which instruct ("write an outline and stick to it"), and gerunds, which suggest action ("forming an online community").

This, from *Foreign Policy:*

The Globalization Backlash
Globalization Means the Triumph of Giant Companies.
 Nonsense.
Globalization Is Destroying the Environment.
 Not really.
Globalization Makes Geography Irrelevant. *Wrong again.*
Globalization Means Americanization.
 Not necessarily.
Globalization Means a Race to the Bottom
 in Labor Standards. *No.*
Globalization Concentrates Power in Undemocratic
 Institutions Like the WTO. *No.*
Globalization Is Irreversible. *Nonsense on stilts.*

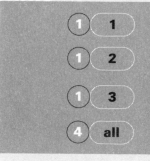

Attention-sustaining devices

Light openings in print

Avoid long, explanatory, throat-clearing openings—and get straight to your main and supporting messages.

Or draw your readers in with a setup that introduces the usual who, what, where, and when, and finishes with a strong point or question.

Geography and the net

The Internet is perceived as being everywhere, all at once. But geography matters in the networked world, and now more than ever.

Brewster Kahle unlocks the cellar door of a wooden building in San Francisco's Presidio Park. He steps inside, turns on the fluorescent lights to reveal a solid black wall of humming computers, and throws out his arm theatrically. "This," he says, "is the Web." It is a seductive idea, but the Web isn't really housed in a single San Francisco basement. Mr. Kahle's racks of computers merely store archived copies of many of its pages, which Alexa, his company, analyzes to spot trends in usage. The real Internet, in contrast, is widely perceived as being everywhere, yet nowhere in particular. It is often likened to a cloud.

Near Collisions Aloft Are Said to Be Rising as Air Traffic Picks Up

"It happened in a flash."

Gilbert Merritt, a federal judge, is describing a flight he took in his twin-engine Piper Navajo last summer. He was near Chicago when suddenly he saw an American Airlines Boeing 727 just a quarter of a mile away, rising quickly toward him. In the next instant, the jetliner banked sharply to avoid a collision, flashing its silver belly at the judge.

"When you see something like that out there, your heart jumps into your throat," Judge Merritt says. The two aircraft came so close that he remembers feeling a bump as the large plane's wake hit him.

Skipping Class 101

Is 8 A.M. too early for you? No problem—just log on and catch up via video

Katrien Naessens remembers feeling sorry for her physics professor last spring as he stood before a nearly empty lecture hall at 8:30 A.M. and proceeded to teach as if the vast room was full. Only about 30 of the 128 registered students showed up.

Her sympathy didn't last long, though. The next morning when her alarm clock went off for physics class, the Harvard junior opted to row on the Charles River instead. Later, the 22-year-old biology major caught up on the lecture not through a classmate's notes—but via the Internet. "It's much easier to sit on your bed in your pajamas and watch the videos on your computer than go to class," Ms. Naessens says.

The Globalization Backlash

Lost your job? Your cultural identity? Your democratic rights? Your clean air and water? Blame globalization—everyone else does. From Seattle to Copenhagen and Washington, D.C., to Genoa, protesters of all stripes and creeds have turned globalization into a shorthand for many of the world's ills. But judging by the widespread misconceptions about the true consequences of the integration of markets, politics, and cultures, a smaller world is not necessarily a smarter one.

The key is to let readers know what they're in for— and to draw them in for more.

inks

Attention-sustaining devices

technique   example

On screen, the
task is the same
as in print:
reveal archi-
tecture and
communicate
content.

A good way to
do this is by
adding a
sentence or two
to a heading,
elaborating a bit
on what it is
pointing to.

Give your
readers enough
to invite them
to view more.

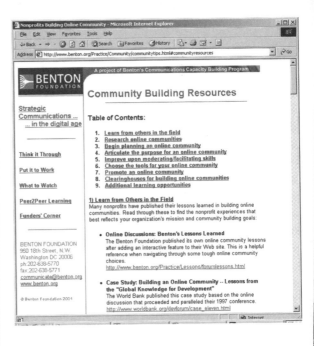

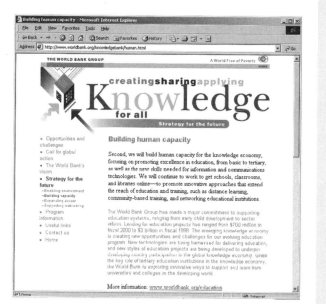

The key is to keep your readers away from what is irrelevant to their interests—and to direct them to what is relevant.

To see how effective your openings are in drawing your readers in, count the click-throughs.

links

1	1
2	9
3	2

Attention-sustaining devices

Revealing headings

Make sure that your headings reveal the structure and content of your argument. Make them communicate, just as your title does.

And these days, it's hard to have too many heads. Especially in writing for the Web, it can even help to have a head for each paragraph (or for each cluster of short paragraphs).

Nine Design Strategies

Define and articulate your PURPOSE

Build flexible, extensible gathering PLACES

Create meaningful and evolving member PROFILES

Design for a range of ROLES

Develop a strong LEADERSHIP program

Encourage appropriate ETIQUETTE

Promote cyclic EVENTS

Integrate the RITUALS of community life

Facilitate member-run SUBGROUPS

The Seven Deadly Sins of E-Learning

1. E-Learning can be used for anything

2. E-Learning is for everyone

3. E-Learning is a technology issue

4. E-Learning is not a technology issue

5. We learn alone

6. Build it and they will come

7. We are on our own

A good way to test your headings is to tape your draft on a wall— confirming the levels of heads and making them parallel in grammatical structure.

links

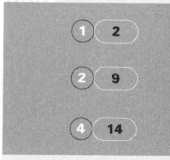

Attention-sustaining devices

Short paragraphs—and sentences

Short paragraphs are less daunting and thus more inviting than longer ones.

And short sentences are less likely to entangle your readers.

Single-sentence paragraphs work especially well in e-mail.

This originally was one paragraph:

China is moving away from a command economy to a socialist market economy—in its own way, doing pragmatic things that Western economists could never have imagined. Township and village enterprises. Strict controls in finance. Dual pricing.

All worked well for the transition from a socialist to a market economy. But the context has changed, with daunting internal challenges, tumultuous external pressures, and more international competition, all requiring speed. And speed means quick, decentralized decision making, which efficient markets can offer. So, to succeed in this fast-paced environment, the government must move even more from providing most goods and services to becoming the architect of a "socialist" market economy.

A market economy, not developed overnight, requires institutions to support it. It requires clear property rights and the enforcement of rights and contracts determining who gets what and when. And it is up to the government to define these rights.

To take advantage of its entrepreneurial people, China needs to clearly define property rights and enforce them fairly and predictably, constraining government interference. How? Through a stronger rule of law.

So was this:

Date: Sat., 20 Jan. 2002 15:03:45 -0500 (EST)
From: Rebecca Kelly <beckyk@cqinet.com>
To: teamcqi-cw@cqinet.com
Subject: Progress report for week of January 15

The course module now opens in a new window, with a set size and no browser buttons. This is a significant improvement, because the previous arrangement confused testers.

We also moved the bottom left-hand navigation buttons to a separate frame, so they can be updated as needed in one file, not on every page.

The bottom left-hand navigation buttons in the course module have been updated with several new buttons. We now have five.

The first button takes you Home by closing the course module window and refreshing the trainee's home page in a new window (with browser buttons).

The second takes you back to Getting Started.

But it's not true, as many assert for the Web, that all paragraphs and sentences must be short to ensure readability.

Longer paragraphs and sentences are fine—if dealing with a single set of ideas.

links

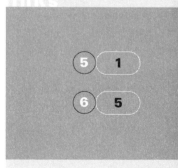

Attention-sustaining
devices

Bulleted lists

Setting off sentences (or phrases) with bullets is another way of relieving the density of long paragraphs.

The technique is most appropriate for introducing the structure and content of text to follow.

It also works well for breaking up a series of long clauses.

In all cases, try to make your bullet points parallel in structure.

Use bullets to introduce the topics you will cover in a chapter or section of your piece. Follow with headings that echo the bullets.

This, from a World Bank report:

Monitor and enforce performance

Ensuring that firms, banks, and individuals live up to their promises is a problem in all societies but tends to be especially severe in the weak institutional environments that characterize many developing countries. Three imperatives for policy are to:

- Develop a strong legal and judicial system, but
- Create incentives to minimize recourse to it, and
- Explore innovative alternative approaches to enforcement.

Develop a strong legal and judicial system. Typically the problem is not the absence of laws but the lack of credible enforcement. Fixing slow and corrupt courts is thus critical for successful economic reform.

Use bullets to describe a process, present examples, make a list, or finish a complex sentence.

This example of a process, from a book on online communities:

The etiquette cycle

In addition to creating ground rules, you'll also need to develop mechanisms for interpreting and enforcing

comment

these rules and evolving them to keep pace with the changing needs of your community. This process can be broken down into three basic and recurring steps:

- You create documents that spell out the ground rules for participation in your community.
- You enforce those ground rules, so that people take you (and the rules) seriously.
- You evolve your ground rules to answer questions, clarify ambiguities, and address emerging social and legal issues.

A list from the same book:

Imposing consequences

There's a range of consequences that leaders can impose on members who violate the community standards. For example, a leader might:

- Restrict someone's participation (gag someone in a chat room, freeze a player in a game).
- Restrict someone's entry to a space (ban a member from a conference, chat room, or game).
- Remove content (Web pages, forum postings, uploaded files).
- Prevent someone from entering the community for some length of time.
- Take legal action (prosecute someone for harassment, fraud, or copyright violation).

Avoid the big consulting firms' practice of using nothing but bullets—and thus destroying the coherence and elegance of your argument.

links

5 10

Attention-sustaining devices

Pull quotes

By pulling into the margin a page's or screen's biggest point, you invite your readers to delve into the text.

That also allows readers to page through your text reading just the pull quotes—on a first pass or as a refresher.

throughs in genetics). They are driving down costs (computing and communications) at a pace never before seen. Leading these transformations are the accelerated developments in information and communications technology, biotechnology and just-emerging nanotechnology.

INFORMATION AND COMMUNICATIONS TECHNOLOGY—CREATING NETWORKS WITH GROWING REACH, FALLING COSTS

The cost of transmitting a trillion bits of information from Boston to Los Angeles has fallen from $150,000 in 1970 to 12 cents today

Information and communications technology involves innovations in microelectronics, computing (hardware and software), telecommunications and opto-electronics—microprocessors, semiconductors, fibre optics. These innovations enable the processing and storage of enormous amounts of information, along with rapid distribution of information through communication networks. Moore's law predicts the doubling of computing power every 18–24 months due to the rapid evolution of

The reason E*Trade is throwing itself into learning the grubby basics of retail is that like many dot-coms, the company is struggling post-bubble. Its stock price has fallen below $15, from a high of $72 just prior to a two-for-one split 18 months ago. And the company trails competitors Charles Schwab and TD Waterhouse in such key metrics as assets under management and average

bureau providing automated on-line securities-transaction services to various brokerage firms. A decade later the company decided to tackle the consumer market, providing on-line investing services for AOL and CompuServe users. And in 1996, E*Trade as we now know it debuted on the Web and on the *Inc.* 500. Christos Cotsakos, the former co-CEO of AC Nielsen, took the helm

'Pushing our brand into the real world is the next evolution,' insists E*Trade's sales and marketing chief.

account size, even though E*Trade spends significantly more than its rivals do on marketing and advertising.

of E*Trade in March of that year.
At the time Cotsakos's move was big news because working at a dot-com was

It's best to stick to one pull quote per page.

ould get up at 4:00 A.M. and rehearse each . At dawn the main test pilot, Scott Anderson, st plane, which was white with high-visibility ng points on the tips of its wings, tail, and ike its motions easy to follow on film. Chase ers, and the occasional jet would accompany lm the test from every angle. Time after time yed the para-ves and spins, overy after a or after a pi-e disoriented nd from level timate engine the FAA will

they can fly high above the storms, ici other kinds of weather that produce bui titudes. They are quieter, for passenger for people on the ground. And they are reliable, because their fewer moving par Indeed, a leading reason for failure is th: ject—usually a bird—has been sucked ti breaking This is wh in which i keys or c into test (full speed part of cen Their grea

The most startling feature of the new SR20 prompted sneering from the rest of the aviation industry: a parachute for the whole plane.

the manufacturers must show that a pilot lane out of a spin. The SR20 met this stan-a combination of spin resistance and the ch would arrest the fall within 1,000 feet andle was pulled—less altitude than planes hen recovering from a spin. sts the company was satisfied that it had a t only would meet the FAA's explicit safety ilso could provide a measure of safety not ible for small planes. The Cirrus pilot would

that turbine engines are safer, very rarely an emergency landing because an engine Cirrus would have loved to race righ ment of an inexpensive "pocket jet," but capital. In the spring of last year the su was startled by the appearance of an en that seemed to have the necessary cash aircraft what Cirrus had done for propell: company, Eclipse Aviation, has an unusu ture, with thirty executives in an office

Two years ago, Harvard started a small department called The Instructional Computing Group that employs several people to videotape about 30 courses per semester and make them accessible to its students over the

It's much easier to sit in bed in pajamas than go to class, says one Harvard student.

university's internal Web site within hours of class. While that is just a small number of all the classes offered, the university says "a good number" of Harvard's undergraduates

1 2

2 7

Attention-sustaining devices

technique	example

People like stories because they're conversational.

And because real people are saying real things, the writing is more human.

Direct quotations (media people call them "quotes," even though quote is a verb) allow you to have a live person support your point.

Indirect quotations do the same, if with less force.

Good quotations can frame an argument effectively while yielding insight into a speaker's character:

✓ There's a general sense, too, that businesses in the modern free market are indifferent to the threats their new technologies pose to privacy. That sense seemed powerfully confirmed in early 1999, when Scott McNealy, the chief executive officer of Sun Microsystems, was asked whether privacy safeguards had been built into a new computer-networking system that Sun had just released. McNealy responded that consumer-privacy issues were nothing but a "red herring," and went on to make a remark that still resonates. **"You have zero privacy anyway,"** he snapped. **"Get over it."**

✓ But, as Robert Ellis Smith and others have pointed out, contemporary notions of privacy have in many cases evolved not despite new technology but because of it. **"Privacy,"** the influential journalist and editor E. L. Godkin famously wrote, in *Scribner's* magazine in 1890, **"is a distinctly modern product, one of the luxuries of civilization."** Phil Agre made a related point to me, a bit more bluntly. **"The idea that technology and privacy are intrinsically opposed,"** he said, **"is false."**

And they lend authority:

✔ The West cannot hope that in a few years Georgian society will unlearn all the bad lessons of many decades, even centuries. **"We'll be walking along the edge of a razor blade,"** Revaz Adamia, a member of the parliament and the head of its defense committee, told me, **"until enough oil is flowing through here to give the West the selfish interest it needs to fight for us. Russia will do everything to destabilize Georgia before that happens."**

✔ Recently I talked with Michael Henry Heim, a professor of Slavic literatures at the University of California at Los Angeles and a professional translator who has rendered into English major works by Milan Kundera and Günter Grass. By his count, he speaks "ten or so" languages. He told me flatly, **"English is much easier to learn poorly and to communicate in poorly than any other language. I'm sure that if Hungary were the leader of the world, Hungarian would not be the world language. To communicate on a day-to-day basis—to order a meal, to book a room—there's no language as simple as English."**

Be sure that your quotations make important points.

Don't quote vacuous phrases that convey little real information.

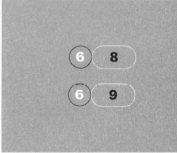

Attention-sustaining devices

Boxes allow you to present a real-life example to support an abstract idea— and give your readers some relief from linear text.

They also allow you to present technical detail that would interrupt the flow of argument.

TECHNOLOGY CAN BE A TOOL FOR—NOT ONLY A REWARD OF—DEVELOPMENT

Technology is not inherently good or bad—the outcome depends on how it is used. This Report is about how people can create and use technology to improve human lives, especially to reduce global poverty.

Some people argue that technology is a reward of development, making it inevitable that the digital divide follows the income divide. True, as incomes rise, people gain access to the benefits of technological advance. But many technologies are tools of human development that enable people to increase their incomes, live longer, be healthier, enjoy a better standard of living, participate more in their communities and lead more creative lives. From the earliest times, people have fashioned tools to address the challenges of existence, from war to health care to crop production (box 2.1). Technology is like education—it enables people to lift themselves out of poverty. Thus technology is a tool for, not just a reward of, growth and development.

Today's technological transformations are intertwined with another transformation—globalization—and together they are creating the network age

BOX 2.1

Technology and human identity

Technology has been at the heart of human progress since earliest times. Our prehuman ancestors fashioned sticks to reach for food, used leaves to sop up water and hurled stones in anger, just as chimpanzees do today. The first human species is named *Homo habilis*—the "handy man". Its fossils from some 2.5 million years ago lie with chipped pebbles, the first unequivocal stone tools. Early *Homo* may have used the perishable technologies of gourds to drink water and leather slings to carry infants. About half a million years ago, *Homo erectus* fashioned elegant leaf-shaped hand axes throughout Africa, Asia and Europe and was apparently using fire. Our own species, *Homo sapiens*—the "wise man" from some 40,000 years ago in Europe, the Middle East and Australia—made tools of stone, bone and antler as well as necklaces for adornment, and drew symbolic art on rock walls— technology in the service of ideas and communication.

Source: Jolly 2000.

CHANGING THE ROLE OF GOVERNMENT

China is moving from a command economy to a socialist market economy—in its own way, doing pragmatic things that western economists could never have imagined, such as township and village enterprises, strict controls in finance, and dual pricing structures.[2]

But the context has changed, with daunting internal challenges, tumultuous external pressures, and more international competition, all requiring speed. And speed means quick decentralized decision making, which efficient mar-

Investing in education and training, in the new infrastructure for information and communication technologies, and in domestic R&D

BOX 1.1

Key elements of a knowledge-based economy

All economies are knowledge-based. What is different, today, however, is that rapidly growing economies depend more on the creation, acquisition, distribution, and use of knowledge. The effective use of knowledge is becoming the most important factor for international competitiveness—and for creating wealth and improving social welfare.

This does not mean that China must simply develop high technology. It means that China must encourage its organizations and people to acquire, create, disseminate, and use knowledge more effectively for greater economic and social development.

The four pillars of a knowledge-based economy are:
- An economic and institutional regime that provides incentives for the efficient use of existing knowledge and, the creation of new knowledge and entrepreneurship.
- An educated and skilled populace that can create and use knowledge.
- A dynamic information infrastructure that can facilitate the effective communication, dissemination, and processing of information.
- An effective innovation system comprising a network of firms, research centers, universities, consultants, and other organizations that can tap into the growing stock of global knowledge, assimilate and adapt it to local needs, and create new knowledge and technology.

The economic institutional regime allows organizations and people to adjust to changing opportunities and demands in flexible and innovative ways. In a sense, it is the fundamental pillar of the knowledge-based economy, since only strong economic incentives and institutions can deploy these resources to productive uses and take advantage of a strong educational base and a highly developed ICT and R&D infrastructure.

Avoid the temptation to use too many boxes—or to use boxes for their own sake, not tied to a major point in the text.

Be sure that your main text refers to each box at least once. And identify the source of boxed material.

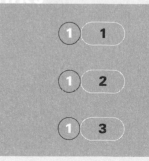

Attention-sustaining devices

Charts, also called figures and graphs, can leave an imprint on your readers' frontal lobes, relieving the relentlessness of text.

It helps to have the title of the chart convey its main point.

It also helps to eliminate all noise, all visual bits that detract from a chart's purpose.

Line chart

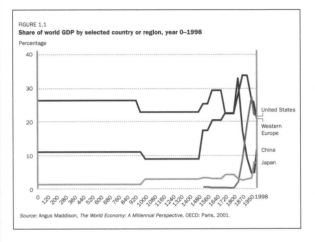

FIGURE 1.1
Share of world GDP by selected country or region, year 0–1998

Percentage

Source: Angus Maddison, *The World Economy: A Millennial Perspective*, OECD: Paris, 2001.

Pie chart

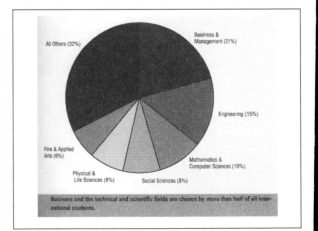

Business and the technical and scientific fields are chosen by more than half of all international students.

Bar chart

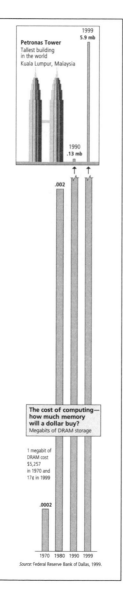

Keep in mind that many readers are self-confessed visual illiterates, so the point of the chart should be obvious and the content easy to gather in.

Ladder chart

Profitable industry— pharmaceuticals top the list

Median return on revenue for
Fortune 500 companies, 1999 (percent)

20
◄ **Pharmaceuticals**

15
◄ Commercial banks

◄ Telecommunications

10

◄ Computers, office equipment

◄ Chemicals
5 ◄ Airlines

0 ——

Source: Fortune 2000.

links

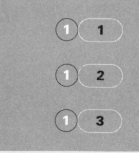

Attention-sustaining
devices

Tables

Tables are useful for direct and precise comparisons of numbers, usually many numbers that would be too cumbersome for text or a chart.

Because tables can be more of a convenience for the writer than an aid to the reader, ask whether your more important numbers might be better presented in a chart, relegating the full set to a lower layer of what you're writing, even to an appendix.

Ideal employers

Companies American MBA graduates would most like to work for

	Rank 2001	Rank 2000
McKinsey & Company	1	1
Boston Consulting Group	2	4
Cisco Systems	3	7
Goldman Sachs	4	3
Bain & Company	5	5
Accenture	6	13
Booz Allen & Hamilton	7	8
Intel	8	12
Hewlett-Packard	9	22
Morgan Stanley Dean Witter	10	9

Source: Universum

Field of Study	1997/98 Foreign Students	1998/99 Foreign Students	% of Total	% Change
Business & Management	100,395	102,083	20.8	1.7
Engineering	71,623	72,956	14.9	1.9
Other (General Studies, Comm, Law)	46,701	49,293	10.0	5.6
Mathematics & Computer Sciences	40,968	48,236	9.8	17.7
Social Sciences	38,849	40,062	8.2	3.1
Physical & Life Sciences	37,201	37,055	7.5	-0.4
Fine & Applied Arts	31,412	31,486	6.4	0.2

Money, money, money

Percentage of companies that had initial start-up capital of

Less than $1,000	16%
$1,000 to $10,000	26%
$10,001 to $20,000	16%
$20,001 to $50,000	10%
$50,001 to $100,000	11%
More than $100,000	21%

Percentage of CEOs that raised start-up capital by tapping

Personal assets	92%
Cofounders' personal assets	36%
Assets of family and friends	33%

Something financial analysts do is to spotlight one number of greatest significance, often with an arrow or bold type.

Red alert
2001 estimates

	Foreign debt as % of exports*	Budget balance as % of GDP	Short-term debt¹ as % of reserves	Current-account balance as % of GDP	Exports to US as % of GDP	Real exchange rate², % change since Jan 1997
China	47	-2.8	11	0.9	4.7	+13
Hong Kong	19	-0.3	11	3.6	28.7	0
Indonesia	186	-4.6	109	2.7	6.0	-43
Malaysia	39	-7.0	20	6.3	23.9	-19
Philippines	108	-3.8	55	9.3	16.1	-32
Singapore	5	1.7	3	21.4	26.2	-8
South Korea	60	-0.4	38	2.8	8.2	-16
Taiwan	24	-6.3	22	3.5	11.2	-14
Thailand	88	-3.0	53	4.7	13.1	-20
Argentina	423	-2.9	96	-3.2	1.0	+15
Brazil	332	-4.7	95	-4.1	2.0	-20
Chile	167	-0.7	44	-2.2	4.4	+4
Colombia	228	-4.4	48	-1.7	10.6	-14
Mexico	93	-0.6	65	-3.6	24.7	+40
Peru	351	-2.2	68	-2.9	3.8	+2
Venezuela	117	-2.7	27	4.7	14.0	+55
South Africa	66	-2.1	268	-0.6	2.6	-30
Turkey	197	-14.5	100	1.7	1.4	+9
Czech Republic	51	-5.2	61	-5.8	2.0	+6
Hungary	87	-2.8	33	-4.4	5.3	+11
Poland	169	-3.6	29	-4.9	0.7	+24
Russia	148	-0.1	39	11.8	3.3	-13

*Goods and services ²2000 ¹Unabsorbed external debt having an original maturity of up to 1 year ²J.P. Morgan trade-weighted index
Sources: Economist Intelligence Unit; J.P. Morgan Chase; The Economist poll.   Figures in red indicate vulnerable levels

links

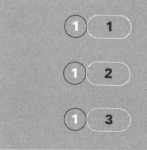

Attention-sustaining devices

Diagrams

Diagrams are good for showing flows in a set of relationships— or stages in a process.

Drawn well, they leave a stronger imprint on readers' memories than straight text.

These, from twin articles on alternatives to traditional utility services:

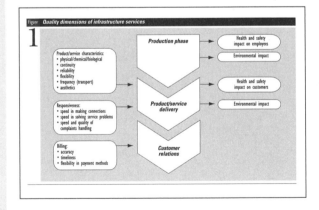

Figure 1 **Why poor customers choose alternative providers**

Poor customers

Do they have access to service provided by the formal utility?

Yes — No

Is the connection charge affordable?

Yes — No

Is the price/quality package attractive?

Yes — No

Main utility provider

Alternative providers

| Low-cost technology | Service flexibility | Payment options | Only alternative |

Figure 1 **Quality dimensions of infrastructure services**

Product/service characteristics:
• physical/chemical/biological
• continuity
• reliability
• flexibility
• frequency (transport)
• aesthetics

Responsiveness:
• speed in making connections
• speed in solving service problems
• speed and quality of complaints handling

Billing:
• accuracy
• timeliness
• flexibility in payment methods

Production phase

Product/service delivery

Customer relations

Health and safety impact on employees

Environmental impact

Health and safety impact on customers

Environmental impact

These, from a cookbook on bread making:

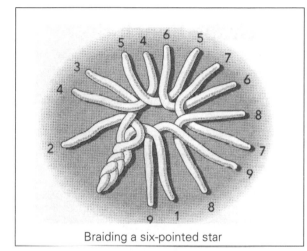

Braiding a six-pointed star

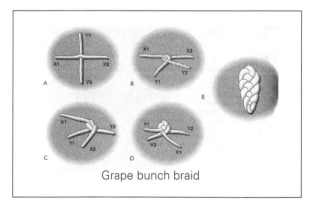

Grape bunch braid

But keep your diagrams simple, testing them on colleagues to see if they impress or obscure.

links

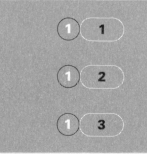

Attention-sustaining devices

technique   example

A face or place is almost certain to catch your readers' eyes.

And today's scanners and digital cameras make it a lot easier to capture images that can reinforce your points.

This, from IBM's 2000 annual report:

This, from a Web site on international
development goals:

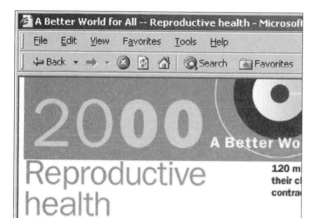

**But use pictures
only to support
your text and
other visual
elements—not
to overwhelm.**

Attention-sustaining
devices

Lightening, layering, and linking are far easier when you work from an obvious structure—with headings that mirror the parts of your argument. An obvious structure also makes it far easier for your readers to retain what you're trying to get across to them.

Deciding on the appropriate structure depends on your topic—and on your audience and purpose. It also depends on the messages you want to convey. Are you dividing a subject into parts? Assembling disparate details into logical groups? Spelling out a sequence of steps, events, or milestones? Identifying a problem, describing its causes and effects, and recommending a solution?

Once you've thought about your audience and purpose, developed your messages, and picked a suitable structure, use that structure to create an outline of content-rich headings—and a detailed plan for what you'll put in each paragraph under those headings.

technique	example

Before writing anything of consequence, come up with answers to five questions.

- **What's your main topic?**

- **Who's going to read what you write?**

- **What's your purpose in writing?**

- **How long should the piece be?**

- **What's your working title?**

Topic?
Specify your topic to define its boundaries and keep your writing from rambling—or unraveling. Avoid generalities and fluff phrases like "an overview of . . ."

❌ Libraries
✅ The future of libraries in the digital age

Audience?
Identify your core and secondary audiences to save time and make your writing more effective. And resist the temptation to tack on groups you would like to reach but probably won't.

❌ People concerned about the future of libraries
✅ Librarians, education policymakers, foundation officials, journalists

Purpose?
What do you want your audience to do once they've finished reading? The answer deserves a place in your statement of purpose, phrased using strong verbs and concrete details.

❌ To inform people about libraries in the digital age
✅ To persuade librarians, education policymakers, and foundations of the importance of libraries as resource centers for new information technologies

comment

Length?

If you've thought well about your audience and purpose, you probably already know how long your piece needs to be. If the average person reads one double-spaced page a minute and you believe your readers will spend twenty minutes reading your work, plan accordingly.

- ❌ However long is necessary
- ✅ 25 paragraphs (10 double-spaced pages)

Pages are merely units of display—paragraphs, units of composition.

Title?

The title is your first chance to engage your readers, so be brief, honest, and communicative. The best titles are memorable and easy to repeat.

- ❌ Libraries in the future
- ✅ Buildings, books, and bytes—Libraries and communities in the digital age

Refine your working title as your writing takes shape. Try to keep your title short, and use a subtitle only if you are adding content and signals essential for your readers.

Most writers dive straight into an outline—or even into drafting—without answering these most basic of questions.

links

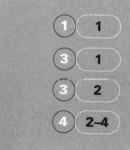

1　1
3　1
3　2
4　2–4

Structures

Start with your main and supporting messages

Your main message is the one sentence you'd give to your readers if that's what you were limited to.

As the most important sentence in what you're writing, it should usually come first.

And it should set up your three or four supporting messages (or points, for short pieces).

Main message

❌ Today's difficult business environment is forcing us to change the way we do things.

✅ Because we're careening toward insolvency, we will cut staff, reduce other costs, slow our payments to suppliers, and get more aggressive in collecting what clients owe us.

Supporting messages

❌ We're going to restructure our three operating divisions

❌ We're going to look closely at all our expenditures

❌ We're going to manage cash inflows and outflows better

✅ In cutting staff, we will favor those who are bringing in the most business.

✅ In reducing other costs, we will stop spending on anything not essential to keeping the lights on.

✅ In slowing payments to suppliers, we will negotiate installment payments spread over several months.

✅ In speeding collections, we will be sure that clients know when they are being invoiced, learn whether they need more information to process payments, and entreat them to pay as early as possible.

Main message

✓ As the U.S. population rises by 72 million over the next thirty years—to 335 million in 2025—more of us will live in the **South and West,** be **elderly,** and have **Hispanic and Asian** roots.

Supporting messages

✓ *Regional.* The **South and West** will add 59 million residents by 2025, with more than 30 million people in just three states: California, Florida, and Texas.

✓ *Demographic.* Also by 2025 the population 65 and older will rise by 28 million people, bringing to twenty-seven the number of states where a fifth of the people will be **elderly.**

✓ *Ethnic.* The **Hispanic and Asian** populations will together gain 44 million people and constitute 24 percent of the total population in 2025, up from 14 percent today.

Amazing is the amount of writing that leaves the main messages unstated—or if stated, not obvious, hidden deep in the text.

links

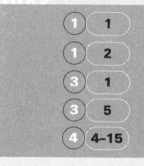

1 · 1
1 · 2
3 · 1
3 · 5
4 · 4–15

technique | **example**

Most pieces of writing have a beginning, middle, and end.

The beginning should present the main and supporting messages.

The middle should have a section heading for each of the supporting messages.

The end can be a brief restatement of the messages, with implications for action.

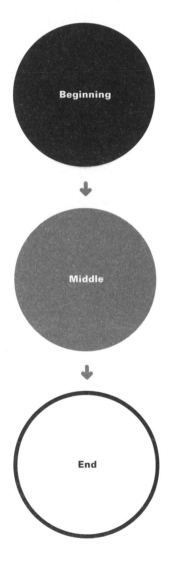

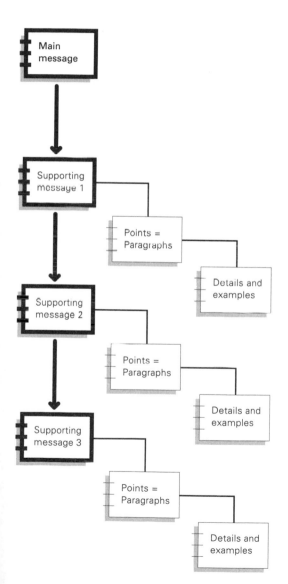

links

As Jean-Luc Godard, the French film director, once quipped, every work of art has a beginning, middle, and end—but not always in that order.

The point: nothing is rigidly fixed when you are developing a line of argument.

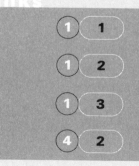

technique   example

Before fleshing out an outline, pick a structure— or several structures— appropriate to your piece.

Although your supporting messages will in most cases drive your main headings, the structures here also suggest lines of argument under each heading.

Divide a subject

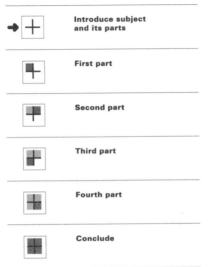

Introduce subject and its parts

First part

Second part

Third part

Fourth part

Conclude

Arrange disparate details

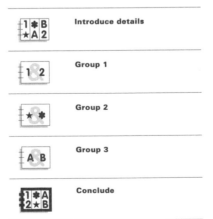

Introduce details

Group 1

Group 2

Group 3

Conclude

comment

Spell out a sequence

▨	**Introduce the sequence**
1	**First step**
2	**Second step**
3	**Third step**
4	**Fourth step**
○	**Conclude**

Solve a problem

⚑	**Identify the problem**
▸?◂	**Describe its causes**
◂◆▸	**Describe its effects**
⦀	**Spell out possible solutions**
!	**Recommend best solution and defend it**

These structures are not ironclad or mutually exclusive—indeed, all but the simplest documents call for variations of the models.

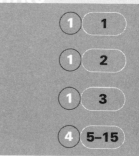

links

1　1

1　2

1　3

4　5–15

Many subjects lend themselves to natural division.

An economy into industries, industries into sectors, sectors into product groups.

A sport into leagues, leagues into teams, teams into players.

A conglomerate into companies, companies into operating units, units into divisions.

 Introduce subject and its parts

 First part

 Second part

 Third part

 Fourth part

 **Conclude**

comment

This outline, from the Commerce Department's *U.S. Industry and Trade Outlook:*

Information and communications
Printing and publishing
Newspapers
Periodicals
Book publishing
Commercial printing

Computer equipment
Personal computers
High-performance computers and servers
Networking equipment

Software and Internet technologies
Systems infrastructure software
Applications software
Enterprise resource planning software
CAD/CAM and CAE
Consumer software
Software development tools
Internet technologies

Telecommunications services
Telephone services
Wireless services

So natural is this structure that it can become a trap that distracts you from other structures more useful for your readers.

links

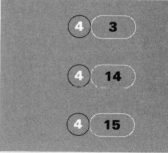

4 3

4 14

4 15

Arrange disparate details in logical groups

Many disparate pieces of information are easier for your readers to digest if arranged in logical groups.

You might group questions and answers into those asked frequently and infrequently, and for those asked frequently into helpful clusters.

Or you might group a change in overall numbers into changes in numbers for different groups, and for those groups into the different reasons for the change.

Introduce details

Group 1

Group 2

Group 3

Conclude

comment

This, from a book on pressing global issues:

20 global issues, 20 years to solve them

Sharing our planet: Issues involving the global commons
¶   Global warming
¶   Biodiversity and ecosystem losses
¶   Fisheries depletion
¶   Deforestation
¶   Water deficits
¶   Maritime safety and pollution

Sharing our humanity: Issues requiring a global commitment
¶   Massive step-up in the fight against poverty
¶   Peacekeeping and conflict prevention
¶   Education for all
¶   Global infectious diseases
¶   Digital divide
¶   Natural disaster prevention and mitigation

Sharing our rule book: Issues needing global regulation
¶   Reinventing taxation
¶   Biotechnology rules
¶   Global financial architecture
¶   Illegal drugs
¶   Trade, investment, and competition rules
¶   Intellectual property rights
¶   E-commerce rules
¶   International labor and migration rules

The idea is to gather what's relevant and to exclude what's irrelevant.

In some ways, this is the obverse of dividing a subject into parts.

The difference is the starting point—from the whole to parts, or from parts to the whole.

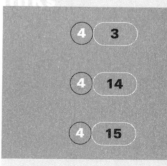

4 3

4 14

4 15

technique   **example**

Sequences are useful when proposing a big menu of things to do.

From that menu, you can cluster the things to do first, then second, then third.

Introduce the sequence

First step

Second step

Third step

Fourth step

Conclude

This, from the Web site of a dot-com:

Our Four-Stage Approach

1. Conceive—Business begins with a concept
¶ Conceive future business and markets
¶ Validate road map for innovation and transformation
¶ Set capitalization strategy
¶ Create market launch plan

2. Design—Architecture follows concept
¶ Construct investment and revenue growth model
¶ Determine technical infrastructure and applications
¶ Draft customer advocacy plan
¶ Design value network relationships
¶ Detail capitalization strategy
¶ Initiate market development

3. Engineer—Set the elements in motion
¶ Develop and test infrastructure and applications
¶ Develop and test customer value experience
¶ Engineer value network relationships
¶ Initiate financial engineering
¶ Launch business

4. Operate—Innovate while you work
¶ Create and monitor performance "dashboard"
¶ Initiate and monitor technical operations center
¶ Implement business reinnovation road map

The key is to make obvious the logic of the sequence to your readers— and especially to make obvious at all times where they stand in the sequence.

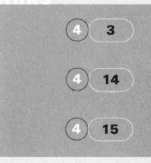

4 3

4 14

4 15

Structures

technique   example

Identify the problem.

Tell readers what you did to learn more about the cause of the problem and its effect.

Then set out what you found.

Given what you found, what are the possible solutions?

Which solution do you recommend— and why?

Identify the problem

Detail the problem

Describe its causes

Describe its effects

Spell out possible solutions

Recommend best solution and defend it

This line of argument, from a white paper on e-learning:

The Elusiveness of Learning Online

Promises unkept—e-learners don't learn

What interviews with human resource specialists show
Little time
Little incentive
Little feedback
Lost opportunity
Lost investment
Lost productivity

Filling the gaps
Make learning part of the work plan
Tie performance ratings and pay to new skills
Blend e-learning with face-to-face instruction

Coming up with individual learning plans

This structure has many varieties—with different orders of problem, cause, effect, and solution, depending on your audience and the urgency of having to act.

links

4 3

4 14

4 15

technique   example

Begin by
introducing the
concept.

Next develop it
in much greater
detail.

Then give
examples of the
concept in
action—starting
simple, getting
more complex.

Introduce the
concept

Go into greater
detail

Develop a simple
example

Develop a more
complex example

Develop an even
more complex
example

Restate the concept

comment

This, from a new textbook on the principles of economics:

Again, an ounce of example is worth a ton of abstraction.

Using Models to Think Like an Economist

Models and predictions
Box and arrow models
Predictions

Models in daily life
Testing an alternative
Strategies for working with models

The puzzle of economic progress
A dismal model
Encouraging evidence

An alternative model of rising living standards
Adding preferences
Adding transformations of physical structures
The growing abundance of physical transformations

Technical progress in agriculture
The external environment for plants
The cellular machinery of plants

Ideas to take away
Models . . .
. . . and optimism

links

Structures

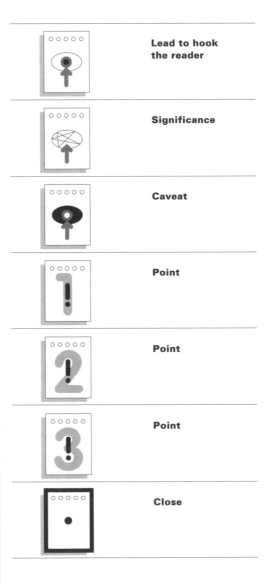

Tell a story

technique   **example**

Perhaps most compelling is simply to tell a story.

Lead to hook the reader

Why? Because people remember them.

Significance

Rather than cold abstractions, stories have observations from life.

Caveat

Point

And rather than mere assertions, they have quotations from live people.

Point

Point

Close

comment

This, from an Associated Press story:

Adoptees Battle Secrecy of Records

¶ Anecdotes about two adopted children trying to find their birth parents

¶ Adopted children seeking birth records

¶ Changes in confidentiality

¶ Opposition to breaking the tradition of confidentiality

¶ Possible compromise: adoptees can be reunited if birth mothers consent

¶ Adoptees oppose compromise

¶ Birth mothers support confidentiality

¶ How one adoptee (from lead) shows the complexity of the issue

¶ How the second adoptee shows that the issue can't be resolved without broader change in social attitudes

¶ Ironic twist that strangers may know more about the adoptee than the adoptee

The typical story has clusters of short paragraphs— often with one making a point, one adding a quotation, and the third giving a comment.

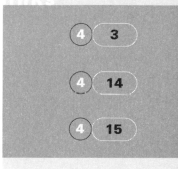

4 3

4 14

4 15

Structures

If your subject is a major event or finding—or if you're worried that you might not hold your readers' attention to the end—rank your information in order of importance, from most to least.

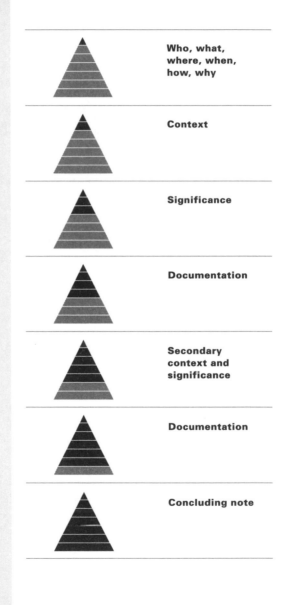

Who, what, where, when, how, why

Context

Significance

Documentation

Secondary context and significance

Documentation

Concluding note

This, from the *Wall Street Journal:*

Three-Drug Therapy May Suppress HIV

¶ A cocktail of three antiviral drugs can force the AIDS virus into hiding, according to new research

¶ The findings cap a ten-year search

¶ The three-drug cocktail would be first major advance since 1987

¶ In tests, the cocktail eliminated 99 percent of the virus detectable in the bloodstream

¶ Director of National Institute of Allergies and Infectious Diseases finds result extraordinary

¶ In another study 24 of 26 patients had virus levels too low to be detected

¶ They also had more infection-fighting CD4 cells

¶ Of less importance are the results of a third study

¶ If findings hold up, as many as 100,000 patients could use the new drugs

Pyramids almost invite readers to stop reading as soon as their interest begins to sag.

That's why journalists get the most basic information to the top.

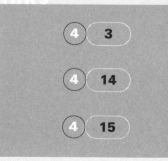

4 3

4 14

4 15

Structures

Readers are interested in the way events unfold—and a chronology encourages readers to stick with your story.

But you need a good story— with plot twists that surprise readers.

And you need signposts to let readers know when events happened.

Introduce
a sequence of
events

Event 1

Event 2

Event 3

Close

This, from the *Wall Street Journal:*

Delayed Impact: 6 Seconds, 2 Dead

¶ Runaway police van careens through holiday revelers on the sidewalk

¶ Woman and infant boy lay dead

¶ Four days later a federal official, Bob Young, is instructed by his boss to help state police

¶ Young hangs up and grimaces: another driver stepping on the gas, not the brake

¶ But over the next three months, he detects a peculiar safety problem affecting tens of thousands of police vehicles

Chronologies usually run from beginning to end.

They can also start with the present, go back, and then go forward.

Or they can run through an hourglass, which merges the pyramid and chronology.

links

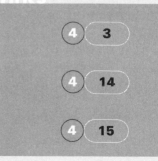

4 3

4 14

4 15

Alternate between general and specific

Bouncing from general to specific and back—offering general observations and comments and providing specific anecdotes—is good for describing changes in people, institutions, and societies over time.

It describes the forces shaping the subject.

It also shows how those forces have played out.

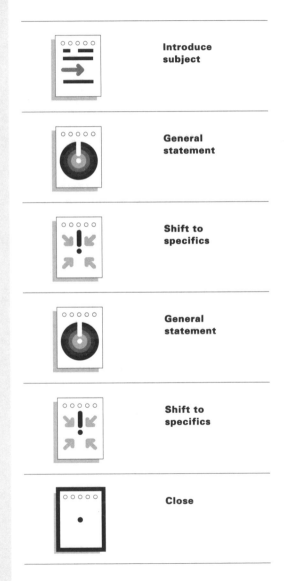

Introduce subject

General statement

Shift to specifics

General statement

Shift to specifics

Close

This story line, from *Governing* magazine:

Will workfare work?

Scene in office in Des Moines where reform program participants came on first day.

How Iowa program relates to national trends, with discussion of issues to be explored.

Closer look at the Iowa program.

What is needed to get welfare recipients into the mainstream of the labor market, not the fringe.

How Iowa program exemplifies contradictory goals.

The alternation allows you to focus on the anecdote— while pointing to broader conclusions.

links

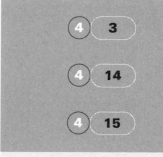

4　3

4　14

4　15

A good outline does two things. It makes obvious to your readers your line of argument. It also reveals the content of that argument.

An approach to reporting and writing features

1. Develop a theme
    What is your topic?
    Who are your readers?
    What do your readers already know?
    What do your readers need to know?
    Write a theme for your story

2. Refine your theme
    Refine your theme—again
    Budget your time

3. Gather raw materials
    What previously published information can you use in your story?
    Who are the experts you should interview?
    Who are the players you should interview?
    Conducting an interview
    Preparing the interview summary

4. Choose quotes
    Be conversational
    Be colorful
    Be punchy
    Let your quotes help tell your story

5. Edit quotes

comment

6. Organize your notes

7. Refine your theme—again
   Budget your time

8. Pick a story structure
   Outline your story structure

9. Write a lead
   Go for the dramatic
   Start a conversation
   Make a promise
   Highlight tension
   Set the scene
   Tell a little story
   Evaluate your lead

10. Write a significance cluster
   The significance paragraph
   The relevance paragraph
   A quote

11. Include any necessary caveats

12. Write the body of your story

13. Write your ending
   Take the reader back to the beginning
   Tell the reader one last story
   Broaden the reader's perspective

Depending on
the length of
what you're
writing, you
might have just
one level of
headings—or
perhaps as
many as three.

links

2 8
2 9
3 2
3 5
4 2
4 3

Assemble a detailed plan

technique	example

Outlines of main and second headings are a great start, but they're also spare and seductive.
 	
People viewing outlines see what they want to see.
 	
That's why it always helps to go beyond outlines to paragraph-by-paragraph plans of the topics you intend to cover.
	The Best Strategies for Building Your Portfolio
	
	¶ Predicting short-term market changes is tricky—so base your investment strategy on diversification and asset allocation.
	¶ Quotation from expert
	¶ Three basic investment concepts
	  • Clarify
	  • Diversify
	  • Review
	
	Clarify your personal goals, timetables, and risk tolerance
	¶ Identify your goals and time horizon
	¶ Time horizon influences decisions about risk
	¶ Risk varies inversely with growth potential
	¶ Allocate to reflect time horizon and risk tolerance
	¶ What kind of investor are you

comment

Diversify among asset classes

¶ Different classes of assets respond similarly to the market, so diversifying protects against volatility

¶ Four classes of assets

¶ Diversification means investing in two and preferably three

   1. Guaranteed annuity plans

   2. Fixed income assets

   3. Equities outperformed others but are volatile

   4. Real estate—a hedge against inflation

¶ Short- and long-term goals

Review and adjust your portfolio periodically

¶ When there are major changes in your life, in the economy, or in the financial instruments available

¶ When the balance of your portfolio no longer reflects your goals and risk tolerance

¶ Transferring funds among accounts

¶ Getting help

Yes, your plan will change.

But you at least have a solid start—especially if you need an OK from a superior or from colleagues writing different parts of a piece.

2	8
2	9
3	5
5	2
5	11

Structures

One of the biggest problems with paragraphs is failing to tell readers the point of what they're reading. Close behind is having a point with no support: a succession of loose, even unrelated, sentences.

The solution to the first problem is simply to add a strong point—and to make it obvious, usually by leading with it. The solution to the second problem is to make sure all sentences bear on the point—and then to unify the supporting sentences by using the traditional rhetorical devices of repeating a key term, counting the elements, signaling what's to come, or changing the structure of the sentences. These devices also make your paragraphs easier to read—and more likely to stay in your reader's mind.

You should make it clear to your reader how each sentence is linked to the point. You can do this by repeating key words and phrases. You can also use transitional words and phrases to enumerate and coordinate a paragraph's sentences. And you can change the structure of your sentences to reveal parallel or subordinate ideas.

Keep them short

Short paragraphs, like short sentences and short words, are easy on impatient readers.	**Short openings** Opening an argument with a short paragraph can encourage the reader to push on for more.

Short paragraphs, like short sentences and short words, are easy on impatient readers.

Use them to deliver your point, to sink a hook, to make a comment, and to provide relief from a succession of long paragraphs.

Short openings

Opening an argument with a short paragraph can encourage the reader to push on for more.

Plenty of entertainment company executives have had high hopes of the relationship between the Internet and entertainment. So what's gone wrong?

Part of the problem lies in delivery. The Internet is pretty good at delivering music and text to customers, but not video, which makes up the biggest slice of the entertainment industry's output. That is largely because video does not work with narrowband connections, and broadband deployment has been rather slower than expected. At the end of 1999, according to *Broadband Intelligence,* an industry newsletter, only around 1.5 million American households, around 1.5 percent of the country, had broadband Internet connections.

Short closings

A short paragraph following a long one can provide a smooth transition to the next phase of your argument.

You can assume one of two things about the teenage boy. You can assume that he is oppressed, depressed, enraged, and endangered, ready to go postal at the slightest provocation. Or you can assume that even after ingesting huge doses of entertainment industry product and processed food, even after being subjected in school to mean teachers and D.A.R.E. courses taught by police officers, even after years of torturing and being tortured by his dearest friends, he still might come through it OK and even think of growing up as having been fun.

In the realm of pop psychology and cultural punditry, the first of these assumptions always wins.

Split a long paragraph into leading and continuing paragraphs

When Mikhail Gorbachev came to power in March 1985, he recognized the harsh economic realities so many of his people knew firsthand: the Soviet economy, after eighteen years of Brezhnev's leadership, was in disarray and did not meet the needs of the nation.

The new leader pushed through a policy of reform that would have two basic thrusts: *glasnost* (the Russian noun for "openness") and *perestroika* (from the Russian verb "to rebuild" or "to restructure").

Believing that *glasnost* would encourage the people of his country to speak out openly about the difficult realities of their daily lives, Gorbachev urged the Communist Party toward restructuring the economy (*perestroika*) so that the Soviet standard of living could be improved.

It's true that a single paragraph shouldn't contain more than one idea; equally true that some ideas deserve more than one paragraph.

Readers breathe (and organize their thoughts) at the end of a paragraph; let them breathe easily.

links

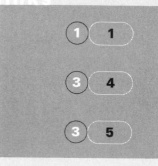

1 1

3 4

3 5

Lead with the topic and point

Powerful paragraphs need more than obvious subjects—they need strong points. Usually stated explicitly at the start, sometimes implied, the point is a statement of opinion or fact.

Support it with other sentences that offer details, examples, and comments.

In the following paragraphs the subject is **bold** and the point *italicized*.

✓ **Wireless technology** *has enormous market potential.* Global cell-phone subscriptions are growing at 35 percent a year, and in the United States, which lags behind much of Europe and Asia, the rate is even higher. The volume of Web transactions that take place on wireless devices will likely grow faster as data traffic overtakes voice traffic.

✓ *For product marketers, the networked* **global economy** *is a mixed blessing.* Companies have benefited from the new sources of low-cost manufacturing, access to huge markets, and the ability to build their brands and to sell directly over the Internet. But as the supply chain spreads across the world and into cyberspace, marketers—from sportswear makers to pharmaceutical companies—become more vulnerable to counterfeiting. Losses to U.S. businesses from global counterfeiting are estimated at $200 billion.

✓ In the constantly morphing technology economy, *video games are the best* **corporate metaphor.** They are all about negotiating fast-moving obstacles and surviving one level to get to the next. Get a good idea, survive all attempts to kill it, and you advance to the next level.

✓ *Real* **politics** *is rather a new thing for Mexico.* For seven decades, Congress was the government's mostly docile rubber stamp. Since winning the lower house last year, the opposition parties have been trying to shape a role both for it and, with a presidential election less than two years away, for themselves. The saga of Mexico's bank bailout—still unresolved, despite a supposed deal last week—has been their first real chance to practice.

✓ *Last year was a magnificent one for* **school vouchers.** Florida introduced a plan to allow children in the worst public schools to move to better schools, private, public, or parochial. Illinois introduced tax credits for educational expenses. In Milwaukee, the model city for school vouchers, where a group of mainly poor black mothers persuaded the city's democratic establishment to experiment, supporters of school choice took over the local school board.

When you lead with the point, your reader can identify it immediately, and a skimmer can pick up your line of argument by reading the first sentence of each paragraph.

links

5 11

technique

example

If all the sentences in a paragraph are about one person, one idea, one country, try using the same noun or pronoun as the subject of each sentence.

In the first paragraph motorists have many names. Confusing. In the second paragraph, they're easier to track.

❌ **Motorists** can be a lonely lot. **They** may get periodic traffic updates along with the news, chat, and music from their car radios. With cell phones, **people** in cars can even talk back to the outside world—asking for directions and apologizing for being late. But, by and large, **drivers** are cut off more than most people from the torrent of information that pervades modern life. And it's a good thing, too, some might say.

✓ **Motorists** can be a lonely lot. **They** may get periodic traffic updates along with the news, chat, and music from their car radios. With cell phones, **they** can even talk back to the outside world—asking for directions and apologizing for being late. But, by and large, **they** are cut off more than most people from the torrent of information that pervades modern life. And it's a good thing, too, some might say.

The first paragraph below uses a variety of verb forms. The second uses only one.

Use a single, simple verb form to express parallel ideas.

❌ Despite their stony homes, corals are fragile creatures. They will be **crushed** if you press too hard on them. If you **cover** them with silt, they can no longer feed on small passing animals. **Blotting** out the light by promoting the growth of algae in the waters above them would cause the other algae, with which they live symbiotically, to lose their ability to photosynthesize.

✓ Despite their stony homes, corals are fragile creatures. **Press** too hard on them and they will be crushed. **Cover** them with silt and they can no longer feed on small passing animals. **Blot** out the light by promoting the growth of algae in the waters above them and other algae, with which they live symbiotically, can no longer photosynthesize.

The three imperatives of the second paragraph unify the three ideas loosely connected in the first.

links

7 7
7 8
7 9
7 10
7 11

Ask a question and answer it

Asking a question in the first line of a paragraph grabs readers' attention and sets up your point.

Using an immediate, direct answer to make your point shows a firm stance, especially when followed by an emphatic.

Whether answered directly or indirectly, questions bring your readers closer to the text by making readers feel part of the discourse.

Immediate answers make you seem—merely seem—unequivocal. They also engage your readers with a conversational tone. And they don't leave the answer to the reader.

✅ **What undermines respect and therefore learning? Hierarchy.** Rigid power relationships can block communication and keep people from behaving authentically toward one another. But hierarchy isn't the same thing as structure. Structure creates clarity; it opens space where people are free to relate to one another. Structure makes learning productive. Hierarchy almost always stifles learning.

✅ **What exactly was Angkor Wat? To the ancient Khmer it was a temple,** a shrine, a mausoleum, an observatory, a public works project, and a source of national pride. It was also a physical representation of Hindu cosmology, a worldview set in stone. The central towers symbolized the mythical peaks of Mount Meru, center of the universe and home of the Hindu gods. The outermost wall represented the edge of the world, while the moat symbolized the oceans.

You can also ask several questions and answer each immediately.

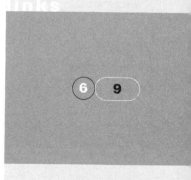

- ✅ **But which countries should represent these regions? India?** Pakistan says no. **Brazil?** Argentina says no. **Nigeria?** Everybody says no. Solutions galore have been suggested: rotating members, tenured members, first-, second-, and third-rank members, members without veto power, dropping the veto altogether, or promising to use it in exceptional circumstances only.

Or answer your question with another question.

- ✅ **Can a woman ruin a man's life? Is there any doubt?** It's the basis of half our favorite romantic myths, from Antony bedazzled by Cleopatra, that serpent of old Nile, to besotted William Hurt manipulated by sultry Kathleen Turner in *Body Heat*. A guy's just going along, being a good Roman general or a tired country lawyer, and suddenly—bam!—there she is, sprawled on a barge or backlit in a white dress on a sticky summer's night, and nothing will ever be the same again.

A series of answered questions can give a paragraph a bantering, argumentative tone.

If you know your readers are going to have reservations about the points you make, phrase them as questions and deal with them directly.

6 9

Once you've rid a paragraph of extraneous material, try repeating a key word or phrase to bind the sentences even more.

Many writers have an aversion to repetition, something they generally acquire in the seventh grade (and in reading Flaubert).

Repeating key terms ties together the sentences of the paragraphs that follow.

✓ It is less than fifty years since we first talked in the United States of the two **sectors** of a modern society—the public **sector** (government) and the private **sector** (business). In the past twenty years the United States has begun to talk of a third subdivision, the nonprofit **sector**—those organizations that increasingly take care of the social challenges of a modern society.

Repeating more than one word can create a resounding echo.

✓ In Europe's first integration at the hands of bureaucratic Roman imperialists these quickening virtues had been stifled, and **therein lay** the seeds of the empire's dissolution. **Therein** too **lay** the kernel of an oblique message for Gibbon's **contemporaries**. And our **contemporaries** too?

Repeating *therein* and *lay* ties the second sentence to the first, and repeating *contemporaries* ties the third to the second.

This is a paragraph that does not repeat its key terms:

❌ A delightful **fairy tale** has taken hold lately in some economic policy circles: the economy is poised for a glorious burst of sustained, sixties-style growth without inflation. It's a **story** told by a spectrum of influential figures, from conservatives to liberal luminaries. Like most good **fables**, this one features a horrible monster who is blocking the path to eternal happiness. That would be the chairman of the Fed, who cannot see that the economic terrain has shifted.

This one does, to bind the paragraph sentences into a coherent whole:

✓ A delightful **fairy tale** has taken hold lately in some economic policy circles: the economy is poised for a glorious burst of sustained, sixties-style growth without inflation. It's a **tale** told by a spectrum of influential figures, from conservatives to liberal luminaries. Like most good **fairy tales**, this one features a horrible monster who is blocking the path to eternal happiness. That would be the chairman of the Fed, who cannot see that the economic terrain has shifted.

Using different terms for the same idea simply to avoid repetition will confuse your reader.

links

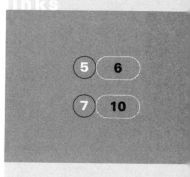

5 6

7 10

Repeat a sentence structure

If sentences are doing similar work, they're easier to understand if they're similar in structure.

Why? Because the reader, spared the effort of processing a new structure, can attend to the words alone.

Indeed, before completing each succeeding sentence, the reader already understands part of its meaning thanks to the repetition of structure.

The supporting sentences in this paragraph do not use parallel structures.

✘ The responses to the White House proposal on nuclear weaponry differed widely. **From Moscow** there was silence. **Leaders in Western Europe** were outraged. And there was a quiet word of support **from Japan's Diet.**

Not unreadable, but not nearly as coherent as:

✔ The responses to the White House proposal on nuclear weaponry differed widely. **From Moscow** there was silence. **From Western Europe** there was outrage. **And from Japan** there was a quiet word of support.

Another example:

✘ *Crash.* Stock market bulls can act as brave as they like, but they cannot deny the terror that this simple word strikes in their breasts. **They may reassure** themselves with talk of record profits or the death of inflation. **All the ways** in which Wall Street's bull run is not like others that ended in tears is something they may point out. **But the stark reality:** stock markets are notoriously fickle and can turn against you at a moment's notice, and this they cannot deny.

comment

☑ *Crash.* Stock market bulls can act as brave as they like, but they cannot deny the terror that this simple word strikes in their breasts. **They may reassure** themselves with talk of record profits or the death of inflation. **They may point out** all the ways in which Wall Street's bull run is not like others that ended in tears. But **they cannot deny** the stark reality: stock markets are notoriously fickle and can turn against you at a moment's notice.

And two more examples:

☑ When the market plunge came, nearly every professional money manager agreed that it was a necessary corrective. **Necessary** to remind investors that most stocks do not double or triple in a year. **Necessary** to prove that, as every investment textbook explains, high returns do not come without high risks. **Necessary** most of all because the capital markets are supposed to be a place where deserving companies get the money they need to grow, not a casino.

☑ Entrepreneurship in the dot-com age remains what it has always been. **Entrepreneurship is about** passion. **It is about** adapting to change without compromising your core vision. **It is about** staying cool under fire. **It is about** being an outsider. But most of all, **it is about** risk.

As with repeating a key word or term, repeating a structure can strengthen the links among your supporting sentences—and between those sentences and your point.

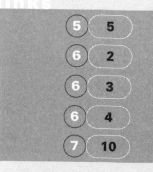

5	5
6	2
6	3
6	4
7	10

Count out the supporting sentences

If you have two or three discrete details to support your point, your reader may absorb them better if you count them out.

Here is a paragraph that does not count out its parts:

❌ The yield on junk bonds did not compensate for their risks. The market was too young to have built up a proper record of likely default rates, especially during a recession. And a large group of junk-bond investors—the savings and loan associations—had an extra leg up into high-yield investment because of federal insurance of their source of cash deposits.

And here is the same paragraph with its parts counted:

✅ The yield on junk bonds did not compensate for their risks, **for two related reasons. The first** was that the market was too young to have built up a proper record of likely default rates, especially during a recession. **The second** was that a large group of junk-bond investors—the savings and loan associations—had an extra leg up into high-yield investment because of federal insurance of their source of cash deposits.

Here are two more examples of counting:

comment

- What does it take to strike a winning Internet alliance? Many of the answers to this question involve classic business principles that are being rediscovered by Internet executives. **First,** be sure to manage expectations of the partnership, so that neither side bets on a miracle. **Second,** don't get stuck in shotgun pairings with companies that have customers or goals that are incompatible with yours. **Third,** make room for revisions, because it's hard to know how companies' strategies and opportunities will change. **And fourth,** be sure that there's a personal bond between the companies that will sustain the alliance.

- What should be done? A first essential is to preserve the **two things** that the National Health Service has done well. **The first** is delivering near–100 percent health coverage for the population. As several countries, most notoriously the United States, are discovering, this is easier said than done; in systems that depend largely on privately financed insurance, it is especially hard. **The second** is the National Health Service's basic cost efficiency: it delivers health care of surprisingly high quality at far lower cost than other rich countries have managed. It is a lot easier to improve things if you start from a position of low rather than high costs.

No mystery here. The count serves the same purpose as initial capitals and terminal periods, signifying the beginning, the middle, and the end of a list or sequence.

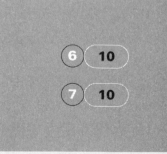

6 10

7 10

Paragraphs

Use conjunctions

If you have three supporting sentences of equal weight, try linking them with *also* and *and.*

X is . . . X is also . . . And X is . . .

Remember to watch for parallel construction.

Note how this pattern can string the details together, injecting pace. Begin by looking for details that start with—or could start with—the same subject and that appear to be of roughly equal importance.

◉ **At first sight the virtues of teamwork look obvious.** Teams make workers happier by giving them the feeling that they are shaping their own jobs. They **also** increase efficiency by eliminating layers of managers whose job was once to pass orders downward. **And,** in principle, they enable a company to draw on the skills and imagination of a whole workforce, instead of relying on a specialist to watch out for mistakes and suggest improvements.

◉ **Germany is generous to immigrants.** For a start, and in deference to their bloodline, it receives each year more than 200,000 Russians, the *Aussiedler* (outsettlers) whose German ancestors moved to Russia two centuries ago. On moral grounds, it takes in any Russian Jews who want to come. It has **also** admitted (in theory temporarily, though it may turn out to be permanently) more than half the entire outflow of refugees from the wars in the Balkans. **And** until three years ago, when it tightened its wide-open asylum laws, it received a good three-quarters of all third-world asylum-seekers reaching the European Union. Beyond that, it is home to some 2m Turkish immigrants originally taken in as "guest workers."

⊘ **The five directors have much in common.** They share major influences—not only Stanislavsky but also Bertolt Brecht and Peter Brook. They **also** turn frequently to modern greats like Ibsen, Chokhov, and Beckett. **And** they are quite often drawn to opera as a way of honing their stage skills.

⊘ **Mediobanca has spun a tight web between the country's main industrial financial groups, leaving little room for others. As well as** 11 percent of Snia, Mediobanca owns a stake in Assicurazioni Generali, Italy's biggest insurer. It **also** owns bits of Ferruzzi Finanziaria and Montedison, its chemicals arm. **And then** there are the bank's stakes in Fiat, Olivetti, Pirelli, Italmobiliare, and GIM.

⊘ **Polaroid jumped into action.** It promoted younger people who, by its standards, would not have been deemed ready for another three years. It **also** looked deep into its organization for up-and-comers it could develop quickly and plug into succession plans. **And** it is now surveying all employees to find out what will make them stay.

Test the unity and coherence of a paragraph by stringing its sentences together with conjunctions.

Feel free to delete them from your finished piece if the connections are just as clear without them.

links

5 6

6 10

technique	example

Transitional words that reveal the relationships between sentences can signal continuation, reversal, concession, and conclusion.

Here's a paragraph with no signals.

❌ The vastness of the project staggers most national governments. Unlike most supersized projects, this one is being paid for with relatively little borrowing. There will be no new taxes, and the government will retain a sizable reserve afterward. The original budget, $21.2 billion, was trimmed this year to $20.3. According to the project coordinator it will probably come in at less than that.

Continuation—*and, similarly, further(more), in addition.*

The same paragraph with its sentences linked:

✅ The vastness of the project staggers most national governments. **But** unlike most supersized projects, this one is being paid for with relatively little borrowing. **So,** there will be no new taxes, and the government will retain a sizable reserve afterward. **Furthermore,** the original budget, $21.2 billion, was trimmed this year to $20.3. **And** according to the project coordinator, it will probably come in at less than that.

Reversal or concession—*or, but, still, despite, even so, otherwise, nevertheless.*

Conclusion—*so, thus, in sum, in short, after all.*

comment

Another paragraph without signals to link its sentences:

Starting sentences with *and* and *but* has been back in vogue since the early 1990s.

❌ Few Britons take much note of Argentina, except on the football field and at *Evita*. There has long been a love-hate relationship the other way. For Britons, the Falklands war was a nasty incident, successfully concluded, that happened sixteen years ago. For Argentines, British rule in the islands is a long-standing, unhealed injury, a theft of their national territory. The war, which claimed more than 1,000 lives, remains a bitter memory. The long relationship between the two countries ensures that in Argentina resentment is mixed with fascination.

The same paragraph, with signals:

✅ Few Britons take much note of Argentina, except on the football field and at *Evita*. **By contrast,** there has long been a love-hate relationship the other way. For Britons, the Falklands war was a nasty incident, successfully concluded, that happened sixteen years ago. For Argentines, British rule in the islands is a long-standing, unhealed injury, a theft of their national territory. **As a result,** the war, which claimed more than 1,000 lives, remains a bitter memory. **In sum,** the long relationship between the two countries ensures that in Argentina resentment is mixed with fascination.

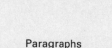

Use bullets

It is difficult to grasp lists of numbers, details, and recommendations packed into a block of text.

Breaking that block into bulleted items clarifies the elements.

Make a general point that you will support with several details of equal weight in no obvious order.

Then set the details off with bullets.

This block of text . . .

✕ The study produced some powerful results. World inequality is very high. In 1993 the poorest 10 percent of the world's people had only 1.6 percent of the income of the richest 10 percent. The richest 1 percent of the world's people received as much income as the poorest 57 percent. The richest 10 percent of the U.S. population (around 25 million people) had a combined income greater than that of the poorest 43 percent of the world's people (around 2 billion people).

. . . reads better as bullets.

✓ The study produced some powerful results.
- World inequality is very high. In 1993 the poorest 10 percent of the world's people had only 1.6 percent of the income of the richest 10 percent.
- The richest 1 percent of the world's people received as much income as the poorest 57 percent.
- The richest 10 percent of the U.S. population (around 25 million people) had a combined income greater than that of the poorest 43 percent of the world's people (around 2 billion people).

comment

Bullets also make the "four tactics" easier to identify and remember.

Setting an element apart makes it easier to remember.

But use bullets sparingly, or they will lose their effectiveness.

☑ In the battle for talent, location is critical. But how can your company compete if it's not based in a hot spot? Professor Richard Florida has identified four tactics.

- *Pay up.* People want work that's challenging, but money matters. Even college graduates won't take a differential to live in a cheaper place.
- *Outdo the competition.* Make your space the hippest one around. Your building and your environment show off who you are.
- *Take the guy with tattoos seriously.* Top talent—especially young recruits— revel in their differentness. That new hire with metal in his ears may be the best thing that ever happened to you. He's a visual cue that you've got an open house for talent, no matter what form it comes in.
- *Invade the backwaters.* Top talent isn't just found at Berkeley, MIT, and Stanford. There are plenty of great people hidden away in the backwaters.

links

3 | 7

Link your paragraphs

Many of the devices that bind sentences within a paragraph can do the same work between paragraphs, creating smooth transitions from one paragraph to the next.

Try repeating a key term, counting the elements, signaling what's to come, asking and answering questions.

Words or phrases from one paragraph repeated at the start of the next explicitly link the two:

✓ **"Wouldn't it be neat if my shoes had springs?"** Every kid who's ever slipped on the high-tops, picked up the rock, and left it all on the court at the end of the fourth quarter has asked that question. It comes up during pregame warm-ups, postgame bus rides, and in sporting goods stores all over the world. It is the natural by-product of millions of young athletes with endless amounts of imagination chasing stardom and glory in their chosen sport.

It's not a new question. Shelves at the U.S. Patent and Trademark Office groan with evidence of failed **attempts to come up with a spring-loaded sneaker** that a factory could actually make. People have been trying to do it for a hundred years. And for the past sixteen years, shoe designers at Nike, a company with a history of brash behavior, seem to have taken it on as a personal challenge.

Turning the repeated word or phrase at the start of the second paragraph into a question raises the eyebrow of doubt or irony.

✓ Many of the EFF's critics predicted this from the start. The move to Washington in the first place was fiercely controversial among its online constituency, whose members worried that the organization would lose touch with its cultural roots.

Cultural roots? It may be hard to imagine something as amorphous and all-inclusive as cyberspace having either roots or a culture. But it does. The chief principle of this culture—decentralization—comes from the structure of the Internet, at present cyberspace's main incarnation . . .

By undermining the point of a preceding paragraph, you can propel your argument in the next:

◯ **In principle, you might expect** "greens" and businessfolk to be at one another's throats. A blind pursuit of profit, say environmentalists, encourages companies to foul up the land, sea, and air. Likewise, few things annoy the average capitalist more than rampant tree-huggers and their ludicrous owl-protecting, business-destroying rules. Across America, businesspeople are cheering the efforts of Republicans in Congress to make a bonfire of green regulations.

    Or so it seems. Yet a strange love affair is growing between some firms and some parts of the green movement. In places such as Washington and Brussels a fast-growing army of business lobbyists is working for tougher laws. Many firms have discovered that green laws can be good for profits—either by creating new markets or by protecting old ones against competitors.

If your paragraphs illustrate a time sequence, use chronology to link them with such words as *At first, Later,* and *Now.*

If a paragraph illustrates a previous point, open it with *For example* or *Consider.*

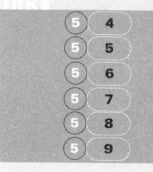

5	4
5	5
5	6
5	7
5	8
5	9

Most writers use three or four basic sentence structures—the simple, compound, and complex sentences taught in all composition books. Then, to give their sentences variety, they commonly multiply the subjects, verbs, objects, phrases, even clauses.

So, how best to move from the common to the uncommon? Think about shortening your sentences. What's too long? Anything more than about 25 words, or about two lines of typescript.

Also think about where best to put each of a sentence's building blocks—each word, phrase, clause. Try to begin separating the movable from the immovable. The embellishments of prepositional phrases, the complications of *that* and *which* clauses, the conditioning by *if* and *when* clauses—these you can move.

And think about looking for patterns to emulate. About using stark attachments—at the front or back of a sentence, or even the middle. About asking the occasional question. The idea is to build an arsenal of sentence patterns that take you beyond the ordinary to the engaging.

Common sentence patterns

You should have a clear sense of the sentence patterns you're using—so that you can begin to branch out to other, more engaging patterns.

Direct

Simplest, and thus clearest, the direct sentence has one main clause and is the starting point for countless variants.

- ✓ The president signed the crime bill.

- ✓ They raise all their own food.

Embellished

The first common variant of the direct sentence is to attach a phrase at the front, middle, or end.

- ✓ After a long legislative struggle, the president signed the crime bill.

- ✓ They raise all their own food on a few acres just outside town.

Complicated

The second common variant is to add a comment or definition with a *which* clause.

- ✓ The president signed the crime bill, which will increase aid to city police departments.

- ✓ They raise all their own food, which allows them to claim farming subsidies.

Conditioned

In addition to embellishing or complicating the main clause, you can condition it with another clause beginning with *if, as, when, since, although, because,* and their many colleagues.

✓ Although doubting its effectiveness, the president signed the crime bill.

✓ Because of their strong belief in self sufficiency, they raise all their own food.

Multiplied

Another variant is to combine the foregoing structures and to multiply their parts.

✓ Although he doubted its effectiveness and feared the consequences of concession, the president gave up the fight and signed the crime bill.

✓ Because of their strong belief in self-sufficiency and despite a hostile climate, they raise all their own food, make their own clothes, and school their children at home.

comment

Notice how the multiplied parts make for long sentences.

One way to simplify such sentences is to search for *and,* deleting unnecessary elements of pairs and series.

links

Leading parts

The structures identified here as stark attachments do more to distinguish the professional from the common than any other pattern.

And all they take is a change in position and the cutting of two or three words.

Type 1

If you have two successive sentences (or clauses) with the same subject, you can cut the subject from one of them, starkly attaching what remains to the other.

❌ **Americans** are struck by an annual outbreak of filial sentiment on Mother's Day. They make more long-distance calls on Mother's Day than on any other day of the year.

✅ **Struck by an annual outbreak of filial sentiment,** Americans make more long-distance calls on Mother's Day than on any other day of the year.

Type 2

If you have a sentence with two or more verbs joined by *and, or,* or *but,* you can drop the verb from one part, starkly attaching what remains to the sentence's front.

❌ The economy **is** undaunted by Mr. Solow's amused skepticism **and has moved on,** and how.

✅ **Undaunted by Mr. Solow's amused skepticism,** the economy has moved on, and how.

comment

❌ The pieces **look** strangely and invigoratingly new **and are** as sleek, fresh, and unassuming as the dancers who perform them.

✅ **As sleek, fresh, and unassuming as the dancers who perform them,** the pieces look strangely and invigoratingly new.

Type 3

If you have a *who* or *which* clause that comments on the subject, you can cut the *who is* or *which is* and attach what remains to the sentence's front, ahead of that subject.

❌ Mr. Law, **who is a former disc jockey,** runs a syndicated phone-in program on SUE, a Sydney commercial radio station, and has 2 million listeners around the country.

✅ **A former disc jockey,** Mr. Law runs a syndicated phone-in program on SUE, a Sydney commercial radio station, and has 2 million listeners around the country.

❌ Nordstrom, **which is famous for an easy return policy and friendly sales staff,** has also built a reputation among fashion retailers.

✅ **Famous for an easy return policy and friendly sales staff,** Nordstrom has also built a reputation among fashion retailers.

By moving an arresting phrase to the beginning of a sentence, you can pique your readers' curiosity about the subject to follow—and vary the structure of your writing.

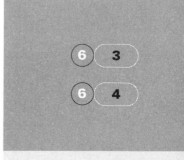

Inner parts

Inner parts are phrases set off by punctuation in the middle of a sentence.

Many writers habitually open subordinate clauses with *which is, that is,* and *who is.* Taking out the pronoun and verb is a standard edit (in the spirit of Strunk and White's "*which-hunting*") and one of the easiest you can make to begin building sentences that are less common.

Type 1

To create a starkly attached inner part, take two sentences that have the same subject, and attach what follows the verb of one sentence as a phrase after the subject of the other sentence.

❌ **Decentralization** itself is neither good nor bad. **It** is a means to an end.

✅ Decentralization, **itself neither good nor bad,** is a means to an end.

❌ **Easter Island** in the South Pacific is famous for its colossal figures carved from volcanic rock. **It** is known locally as Rapa Nui.

✅ Easter Island in the South Pacific, **known locally as Rapa Nui,** is famous for its colossal figures carved from volcanic rock.

Type 2

You can do the same with part of a compound predicate, turning it into a phrase or dependent clause after the subject. (Look for a subject with two or more verbs joined by *and, or,* or *but.*)

❌ And South Korean conglomerates **are taking** advantage of well-honed marketing skills **and have altered** their export patterns.

✅ And South Korean conglomerates, **with well-honed marketing skills,** have altered their export patterns.

comment

❌ The old record **was** 22 hours and 26 minutes **and was** established on April 24–25, 1953, by Oregon Senator Wayne Morse in a filibuster against the tidelands bill.

✅ The old record—**established on April 24–25, 1953, by Oregon Senator Wayne Morse in a filibuster against the tidelands bill**—was 22 hours and 26 minutes.

Type 3

Removing *who is* or *which is* picks up the cadence by attaching the elaboration starkly.

❌ Morgan Stanley's Mary Meeker, **who is** one of the computer industry's most respected analysts, reckons that the Internet has the potential to become even bigger.

✅ Morgan Stanley's Mary Meeker, **one of the computer industry's most respected analysts,** reckons that the Internet has the potential to become even bigger.

❌ Glasgow, **which is** celebrated for its grand buildings erected during its heyday as a commercial hub of the Victorian era, is the United Kingdom's "City of Architecture and Design" this year.

✅ Glasgow, **celebrated for its grand buildings erected during its heyday as a commercial hub of the Victorian era,** is the United Kingdom's "City of Architecture and Design" this year.

Many writers also introduce examples with *such as, for example, that is,* **and the shorthand** *i.e.* **and** *e.g.*

Dropping those openings can quicken the pace of your sentences.

6   2

6   4

technique   **example**

As with leading parts and inner parts, you can use starkly attached trailing parts to vary the rhythm of your writing and increase its input.

Type 1

Again, the cue for this change is two successive sentences (or clauses) with the same subject.

❌ **The deep, intrusive past** was never far away. **It** was echoed in a ruin, a habit, a village, a sight not meant to be a reminder but there all the same.

✅ The deep, intrusive past was never far away— **echoed in a ruin, a habit, a village, a sight not meant to be a reminder but there all the same.**

❌ **His parents** contracted with a local printer for 5,000 copies. **They** paid the bill with money from the family's unused college savings.

✅ His parents contracted with a local printer for 5,000 copies, **paying the bill with money from the family's unused college savings.**

Type 2

You can also convert part of a compound predicate to a phrase at the end. The cue is two or more verbs joined by *and, or,* or *but.*

❌ The Washington Post's Metro section **covers** the D.C. metropolitan area **and leaves** national headlines to the front page.

✅ The Washington Post's Metro section covers the D.C. metropolitan area **leaving national headlines to the front page.**

❌ In the city and on Wall Street he **was** an impeccable dresser **and was** besuited by English tailors.

✅ In the city and on Wall Street he was an impeccable dresser, **besuited by English tailors.**

Type 3

As with some inner parts, you can remove the *who is* or *which is* from a dependent clause and attach the remaining phrase at the end with a dash or comma.

❌ He never tired of reminiscing about the fourteen months he lived among the Wachagga, **who are** a sophisticated tribal people who grow coffee on the slopes of Mount Kilimanjaro.

✅ He never tired of reminiscing about the fourteen months he lived among the Wachagga, **a sophisticated tribal people who grow coffee on the slopes of Mount Kilimanjaro.**

❌ Renewable energy has long been hopelessly more expensive than energy produced by the fossil fuels, **which include** coal, oil, and gas.

✅ Renewable energy has long been hopelessly more expensive than energy produced by the fossil fuels—**coal, oil, and gas.**

Compound predicates can be wearying, lulling readers into indifference.

Keep them hooked by converting the best part of a long predicate into a stark attachment.

links

6 2

6 3

Occasional short forms

technique	example
Most writers produce successions of long sentences, 30, 40, 50 words long. **Try giving your reader some relief with a 5-to-10-word sentence.**	**Fragment** Sentence fragments, disallowed by rigid writers and grousing grammarians, mimic speech. Unexpected, they command attention, so you should draw that attention to big points and comments. ✅ The world has changed. **So have our views of the state.** ✅ The marriage of America and the rest of the world is just that—a marriage. **For better and for worse.**
Use a fragment to answer a question, change direction, or get attention.	Fragments often work well in answering a question. ✅ How effective are our schools in delivering even basic education? **Not very.**
Remember, though, to blend the short with the long.	**The short sentence—to start a paragraph** Use it to open an argument with a strong point, or shift to something new. ✅ **But it is wrong, all wrong.** The idea that thought is the same thing as language is an example of what can be called a conventional absurdity: a statement that goes against all common sense but that everyone believes because they dimly recall having heard it somewhere and because it is so pregnant with implications.

⊘ **Lack of housing is another problem.** More than a billion people live in inadequate housing, and about 100 million are estimated to be homeless worldwide.

The short sentence—to finish a paragraph

Finish a paragraph with a short declarative sentence to reinforce your point, put it in a broad perspective, or build a bridge to the next paragraph.

⊘ Given the speed with which women's businesses are growing, it is doubtful that they need so much government activism to help them. **Politically, though, it makes sense.**

⊘ It is true that Mr. Bush does not have Bill Clinton's formidable ability to process ideas and information. **Few do.**

Pairs and trios

Two or more short sentences set apart ideas that would otherwise be more closely linked by a conjunction in a single sentence.

⊘ **Yes, we can use the big words. The president has already used them.** And perhaps we had better get used to using them again.

⊘ **I came. I saw. I conquered.**

> The strongest positions for the short sentence are the beginning and end of a paragraph— especially at the beginning or end of a piece.

links

3 6

5 4

6 6

7 11

Sentences

Dramatic flourishes

Flourishes—from unusual punctuation highlighting a word or phrase to unusual word order—can add drama to an otherwise common sentence.

Interruptive dashes

You can occasionally use a dash to separate part of a sentence and thus draw attention to it, just as you would with a dramatic pause in speech. The dash forces your readers to momentarily reflect on what precedes the dash—and then flings them into what follows.

- America welcomed—**and China criticized**—a decision by Israel to cancel the sale of an early-warning radar system to China.

- Entrepreneurship is about being an outsider—**and about taking risks.**

Imperatives

Using the imperative is like voicing a command. Spare use grabs attention. Overuse slides into the dictatorial.

- **Beware** of all enterprises that require new clothes.

- **Ask** stupid questions. Growth is fueled by desire and innocence. Imagine learning throughout your life at the rate of an infant.

comment

Recasts

The recast takes the general and makes it more specific, adding power and clarity that neither could achieve on its own.

● All art is in a sense symbolic; but we say "Stop, thief" to the critic who deliberately transforms an artist's subtle symbol into a pedant's stale allegory—**a thousand and one nights into a convention of Shriners.**

Reversals

The reversal adds to the power of what you mean by stating the same idea negatively and then positively, or sometimes vice versa. The negative to positive is stronger because it sets up an expectation.

● **It's not just that** a woeful lack of imagination makes us want to reincarnate everything in our own image. **It's that** we have lost, in our secularized age, the vocabulary of transcendent Good and Evil.

Inversions

The inversion changes common sentence order to shift a word or group of words to the emphatic opening slot.

● **True partners they are,** but the French still have a way of making the Germans sweat over Europe.

By scanning advertising copy for engaging flourishes, you can get a sense of how to apply such touches to your own writing—and how irritating they can be when used to ingratiate or manipulate, or simply when overused.

links

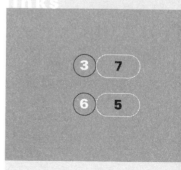

Elegant repetitions

Repetition—avoided far too often—can be a powerful rhetorical device.

It can bring order and balance to a sentence's parts.

And it can deliver more impact than inelegant variation ever could.

Word

Repeating a word increases its power in the sentence by forcing the reader to reconsider its meaning and that of the words it frames or modifies.

✓ There is practically **no** work, **no** money, **no** hope, and seemingly **no** effort.

Root

Repeating the root of a word signals different meaning and links two ideas more strongly than otherwise. But be sure you're not just being cute.

✓ **Disrupted** and **disruptive,** as ornery and independent as Mel, "Far North" breaks away from order to move through **disorder** to older, deeper **orders.**

Prefix or suffix

Repeating a prefix or suffix does more than show that words are doing the same work. It forces the reader to see their association.

✓ **Dis**tance no longer delays **dis**covery, as technology has brought near what had been far.

✓ But more important than the lobby**ing**, and the worry**ing**, is the failure of public debate on prison, its costs, and the alternatives.

Preposition

A special case of repeating a word, a repeated preposition separates what otherwise would be the many objects of one preposition, emphasizing that they are more separate than joined.

 Our big brass horns, our huge noisy drums and whirring violins make a flood of melodies whose poignancy is heightened **by** our latent fear and uneasiness, **by** our love of the sensual, and **by** our feverish hunger for life.

Sound

Alliteration, repeating a sound at the beginning of two or more words, can add poetry to the ordinary.

 Fatter capital ratios, **fancy** risk-management systems, and **faster** diversification: all of these things are undoubtedly creating a **fitter** banking system.

Structure

For the parts of sentences doing the same work —signaled by the conjunctions *and, or, but*— repeating the structures adds balance.

 Ordinary people may not dine in three-star restaurants, **but they have** enough to eat; **they may not** wear Bruno Maglis, **but they do** not go barefoot; **they may not** live in Malibu, **but they have** roofs over their heads. Yet it was not always thus.

But as with any device, don't overdo it.

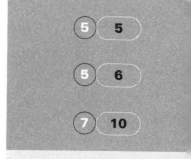

links

5	5
5	6
7	10

Sentences

Credible quotations

technique   example

Quotation offers relief from exposition.

It is also far more engaging, perhaps explaining why readers attend to the speech-laden prose of a novel far longer than a piece of expository writing.

Set up your quotations by summarizing basic information and letting the quoted authority deliver a colorful punch line that tells the reader something new or clarifies an important point.

Direct quotation

Notice how frequently the *Wall Street Journal* brings people into its stories with a quotation and the effect on the credibility of argument. Suddenly, it's no longer up to the writer to persuade. It's up to the chosen authority.

✓ It's no surprise that Warhol did the guest-star stunt—**Halston once observed** that Warhol "would go to the opening of a drawer."

✓ "Trusting the government with your privacy," **snorted *Wired* magazine,** "is like having a Peeping Tom install your window blinds."

Indirect quotation

Indirect quotations do not guarantee exact wording but they still command the authority quoted. Using variants of such constructions as *says that*, without quotation marks, indicates the looseness of the quotation.

✓ First, **the pundits say,** Microsoft has conquered all the easy ground already: as its traditional markets become saturated, growth will become slower and less profitable.

✓ **Toyota says that** it needs to produce 3m vehicles a year in Japan if it is to keep its domestic workforce at existing levels.

- **She once told** an interviewer **that** her Olive Oyl voice was an attempt to imitate the actress Zazu Pitts.

Opening with a quotation

Opening an entire piece with a quotation sets the tone for all that follows.

- **"Unsex me!"** cried Lady Macbeth in a plea to the spirits that should probably be inscribed in the Pentagon somewhere.

- **"The source of my painting is the unconscious,"** Pollock declared, and there was no Abstract Expressionist of whom this was more clearly true.

- **"I still have arms and legs and I still have my smarts,"** says Gloria Mason, a 73-year-old widow from Wheaton. "Where do I go?" Every morning, millions of men and women—smart, curious, vibrant—face a day with no deadlines, no demands, no schedule.

Look for quotes that sound like speech, that entertain or amuse, and that express one or two straightforward ideas.

Make sure each quotation advances your story rather than restates what you've already written.

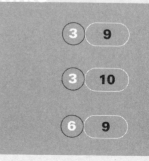

Conversational injections

Like the quotation, conversational injections bring a bit of personality into what would otherwise be impersonal and formal.

They range from wry comments to the questions and contractions that populate speech.

Like flourishes, conversational injections should be used stingily. Don't go overboard.

Comments

Some words and phrases, slipped in at various points in a sentence, can reveal more of your view than mere declaration, injecting a personal touch and drawing you closer to your reader.

- Son of one Revolutionary War hero and son-in-law of another, Allan Melvell had, **as we would say today,** good connections.

Questions

Questions address readers, engaging their attention. They can also add twists to an otherwise sober discussion. But don't sprinkle them indiscriminately—for no effect. They work best at the beginning or end of a paragraph, creating bonds with paragraphs that precede or follow.

- **Remember** when Japanese cars were cheap and nasty**?**

Questions answered

Many writers open a paragraph with a question and keep the reader musing about possible answers through to the end. Fine, if that's the desired effect. More potent, however, is the immediate answer, especially with a fragment.

- Does all this seem overdone? **Well, yes.**

Parenthetical asides

Asides plug in an idea not directly related to the main idea. They can also make it easier for readers to make the leap from subject and predicate or to navigate the elements of a series.

> ✓ The most pathetic example is Abkhazia, once **(give or take a few cockroaches)** the Côte d'Azur of the Soviet Union.

Slipped-in modifiers (often as asides)

Some writers put a modifier in parentheses to offhandedly highlight something about what's being modified.

> ✓ So researchers have gone back to the drawing board and are searching for suitable **(and suitably cheap)** substances among the castoffs from antiviral drugs used to treat AIDS in rich countries.

Contractions

Contractions once were all but forbidden in formal writing. Then, in the mid-1980s, they began to appear in the news—and since, more broadly. Conversational, they imbue sentences with an (often needed) air of informality.

> ✓ Given this climate, **it's** hardly surprising that Satan should have metamorphosed from a pitchfork-wielding fiend into the Armani-clad guy next door.

Check your injections by making sure each one advances your story.

links

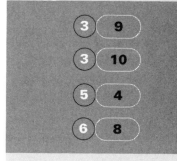

3	9
3	10
5	4
6	8

Sentences

Deft connections

Much of writing is connecting words and phrases that are doing the same work—multiple subjects, verbs, modifiers, objects.

And most writers connect them with conjunctions and commas in common ways.

Here are some uncommon connections.

Series from short to long

Rearranging elements of a series from short to long and from simple to compound makes them easier for readers to understand. Start by counting the syllables of each word—and the words of each phrase—and try arranging them from short to long.

- They're **smart, ambitious,** and **uncomplaining.**

Compare this with the less orderly *ambitious, smart,* and *uncomplaining*—and with *uncomplaining, ambitious,* and *smart,* inverted for an emphatic, monosyllabic finish (which would be even more emphatic without the *and*).

Series without a conjunction

Dropping a conjunction creates a series that is not exhaustive, but a mere sampling of possibilities. It also makes your reader see the parts of the series as more separate than joined.

- Mention the "new economy" and what comes to mind? For many people, **dot-com companies, fancy Web sites, piles of cash.**

- The other passengers **hung their heads, consulted their watches, worked their jaws** frantically over thin bands of flavorless gum.

comment

Starting with a conjunction

An obvious way to break a long sentence or two or three independent clauses is to make each clause a sentence.

✓ They can pull back now, lose their early-mover advantage, and let others work out how the Internet can become an entertainment medium. **Or** they can go on pouring billions of dollars into what, so far, has proved to be a very interesting drain.

✓ Farmer and Kim were upstarts, mere clinicians, and their message was embarrassing to many people there. **But** they had solid data. **And** some of the people who had received their data at the meeting were, after all, scientists.

Parallel constructions

Parallel structures intensify the bond between two of a sentence's joined parts and make the sentence easier to read. Any conjunction is a signal for attending to parallel structure.

✓ Greenspan stressed the need **for governments to regulate** their financial systems adequately, **for governments and the private sectors to provide** investors with full and timely economic and financial information, **and for governments not to insulate** investors from risk by bailing them out when times become tough.

The connectors you use— conjunctions, punctuation, transitional phrases— allow readers to process information quickly by establishing relations among sentence parts.

links

5 8

5 9

7 9

7 10

technique   **example**

Sentences can get off to a faster start with a one-syllable opening than with words of two or more syllables.

And occasionally successions of one-syllable sentence openings can bind a paragraph more tightly.

It

An opening *it* can get a paragraph or entire piece off to a fast, emphatic, monosyllabic start.

- ✅ **It** is often easier to kill an organization than to change it.

- ✅ **It's** good to be nosy, to inquire, to be as critical as possible before you give your money or your time.

There

Opening with *there is* or *there are* is one of the most natural ways of starting a sentence in speech and thus in print. So natural that it tires from overuse.

- ✅ **There** wasn't damage; **there** was devastation.

- ✅ With his droopy moustache, **there's** no mistaking him.

This

As a pronoun for something that has just been mentioned, or is about to be, *this* is a useful monosyllable for opening a sentence.

- ✅ **This** is a good day to take a close look at a famous speech.

- ✅ **This** would be wizardry indeed.

That

As a pronoun for something that has just been mentioned or is about to be, *that* is another useful monosyllable for opening a sentence.

✓ Stock market observers say the economic turbulence will be set off by many companies buckling under the weight of excessive debt. **That** scares the pinstripes off the pants of some who heed the bond market's signals.

✓ **That** will teach them to disrespect their bodies.

What

As a pronoun directing attention to the statement about to be made, *what* captures the reader's attention.

✓ **What** a shock it must be for Koreans to discover that what they thought was a rich, rapidly growing homeland with near-perfect job security is in fact teetering on the edge of bankruptcy.

✓ **What** they didn't know proved liberating.

Starting a sentence with **it** *is generally to be avoided, however, as in such constructions as* **It is Johnson who damaged . . . , It can now be stated with certainty that . . . , or It goes without saying that . . .** *(why say it?).*

links

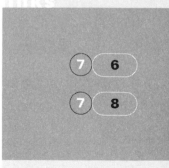

7 6

7 8

Many words and phrases, while grammatically and syntactically correct, add little for your readers and often detract. You can identify many problematic words and phrases by searching (or scanning) for *and, -ed, of, which,* and *-ion*—each a red flag for editorial action.

You can then take action by trimming fat, clarifying pronoun references, and using the active voice.

Indeed, that is how this chapter is arranged—first presenting the red flags, to see the edits they suggest, then suggesting edits to make your writing clear, concise, precise.

Keep in mind, though, that there are no rules of editorial style, only preferences. So consider the remedies here tips, not rigid rules.

The conjunction *and* allows you to join words, phrases, and clauses—and thus to stuff more than you might need into a sentence.

By searching for *and* you can remedy many of the problems it causes.

You can do the same by scanning a document on screen or paper.

Trim a word or phrase

❌ inherent **and** inalienable rights

✅ inalienable rights

Break a long sentence into two or more sentences

❌ The speaker, though he paid $15,000 to attend the conference, probably felt that the egg on his face was not worth it, **and he** must still be wondering how a person once all-powerful could have been subjected to such ignominy.

✅ The speaker, though he paid $15,000 to attend the conference, probably felt that the egg on his face was not worth it. **He** must still be wondering how a person once all-powerful could have been subjected to such ignominy.

Make phrases parallel

❌ Aides on Capitol Hill talk about *running the country* **and** *the manipulation of constituents.*

✅ Aides on Capitol Hill talk about **running the country** and **manipulating constituents.**

Arrange pairs or series from short to long

❌ *Pieces of eight, Venetian ducats,* **and** *doubloons* poured to the floor.

✅ **Doubloons, Venetian ducats,** and **pieces of eight** poured to the floor.

Convert one of two clauses to a leading part

❌ **Americans are struck by** an annual outbreak of filial sentiment on Mother's Day, **and they make** more long-distance calls on Mother's Day than on any other day of the year.

✅ **Struck by an annual outbreak of filial sentiment, Americans make** more long-distance calls on Mother's Day than on any other day of the year.

Convert what follows one of the verbs to a leading part

❌ She **is** pragmatic and determined **and has** plenty of experience helping run opera houses in Britain and France.

✅ **Pragmatic and determined, she has** plenty of experience helping run opera houses in Britain and France.

You can also search or scan for other single conjunctions *(or, but)* and for such double conjunctions as **neither . . . nor** and **not only . . . but also.**

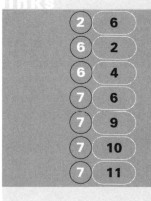

2	6
6	2
6	4
7	6
7	9
7	10
7	11

Words and phrases

technique

example

Many words ending in **-ed** are nouns *(reed)* or past tenses of verbs *(revered)*.

But many others are past participles following some form of the verb *to be (is, was, will be, are, were).*

Examples include *contained, located, conducted, learned.*

Trim fat

When the *-ed* word is in a clause modifying a noun, delete it.

- ✖ People *who are located* in towns
- ✖ People *located* in towns
- ✔ People in towns

- ✖ A study *that was conducted* by Bain & Company
- ✖ A study *conducted* by Bain & Company
- ✔ A study by Bain & Company

- ✖ lessons learn**ed** from four years
- ✔ lessons from four years

Simplify an adjective

- ✖ centraliz**ed** control
- ✔ central

- ✖ industrializ**ed** countries
- ✔ industrial countries

Switch to a comparative adjective

- ✖ increas**ed** effort   ✔ **more** effort
- ✖ improv**ed** results   ✔ **better** results
- ✖ enhanc**ed** returns   ✔ **larger** returns
- ✖ reduc**ed** profits   ✔ **lower** profits
- ✖ is preferr**ed** to   ✔ is **better** than

comment

Switch from passive to active voice

When the *-ed* word is followed by *by*, the voice is passive, which you should usually convert to the active.

Transpose the actor and what is acted on

❌ *That book* was publish**ed by** Knopf.

✅ **Knopf published** that book.

Inject an actor

❌ The Gettysburg Address was deliver**ed** in November 1863.

✅ **Lincoln delivered** the Gettysburg Address in November 1863.

But leave the voice passive if what is acted on is more important than the actor.

Switch from participle to verb

❌ is engag**ed** in

✅ **engages** in

Switch from passive to leading gerund (*-ing*)

❌ The election of new civilian governments at municipal, state, and national levels was capp**ed** by the election of Olusegun Obasanjo as president.

✅ **Capping** the election of new civilian governments at municipal, state, and national levels was that of Olusegun Obasanjo as president.

Past participles are one of the main things to look for in beginning to tighten your writing.

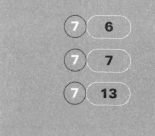

7 6

7 7

7 13

Words and phrases

technique   **example**

Search or scan a document for *of* **and try to delete it and its companion** *the.*

Superfluous nouns

✖ **The purpose of** this report is to review . . .

✔ This report reviews . . .

✖ **The level of** demand for chips fell in the third quarter.

✔ Demand for chips fell in the third quarter.

✖ **The issue of** candid disclosure is receiving more attention from the SEC.

✔ Candid disclosure is receiving more attention from the SEC.

Here are several more superfluous nouns that you can often delete along with *the* and *of*.

the amount of	the idea of
the area of	the magnitude of
the case of	the nature of
the character of	the number of
the concept of	the presence of
the degree of	the process of
the existence of	the sum of
the extent of	the volume of
the field of	the way of

Nouns unnecessarily propped up
❌ **the** production **of** steel
✅ producing steel

❌ **the** assembly **of** computers
✅ assembling computers

Nouns separated from an indefinite adjective
❌ some **of the** countries
✅ some countries

❌ many **of the** e-learning companies
✅ many e-learning companies

Switch to the possessive
❌ the contents **of the book**
✅ **the book's** contents

❌ the future **of the industry**
✅ **the industry's** future

Sometimes these
edits change
a sentence's
meaning, so take
care that they
leave your
intent intact.

links

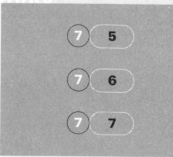

7 5

7 6

7 7

Words and phrases

technique   **example**

Which is useful for connecting your sentence parts—if it's not misused.

So search or scan for *which* to identify and remedy possible problems.

Often you can cut the clause *which* is connecting.

Often you can cut the *which*.

And if the clause defines the noun it follows, switch the *which* to *that*.

Delete the *which* clause

❌ The main problem, **which** remarkably few writers are aware of, is failing to set off a dispensable clause by punctuation.

✅ The main problem is failing to set off a dispensable clause by punctuation.

Delete *which* and its verb

❌ A good solution, **which is** known as ellipsis, is to delete the *which* and the auxiliary verb—**which is** a solution that works best with *is* and *are*.

✅ A good solution, known as ellipsis, is to delete the *which* and the auxiliary verb—a solution that works best with *is* and *are*.

Pull part of the *which* clause to the front of the sentence

❌ The software, **which the company just released,** is likely to be a big improvement.

✅ **Just released,** the software is likely to be a big improvement.

comment

Punctuate a *which* clause

 The new software **which** the company has been developing since 1999 is now available.

 The new software, **which** the company has been developing since 1999, is now available.

Switch to *that* for defining clause

 The software **which** the company just released is likely to be a big improvement.

 The software **that** the company just released is likely to be a big improvement.

Strunk and White, in their *Elements of Style*, advise writers to go *which*-hunting, presumably because of the many unintentional misuses.

links

7 6

7 12

Search for *-ion*

The *-ion* ending signals a word that may be too long, too vague, or simply too obscure for your readers.

By searching or scanning for *-ion*, you can decide whether to switch to something shorter, cleaner, more obvious.

Switch from Latinate abstractions to Anglo-Saxon equivalents

- ❌ nictitation
- ✅ wink

- ❌ motivation
- ✅ drive

- ❌ pollution
- ✅ smog, smoke, effluents

- ❌ conflagration
- ✅ fire

- ❌ origination
- ✅ source

- ❌ initiation
- ✅ start

- ❌ utilization
- ✅ use

- ❌ population
- ✅ people

- ❌ termination
- ✅ end

- ❌ proportion
- ✅ part (or share)

- ❌ remuneration
- ✅ pay

- ❌ conclusion
- ✅ end

Switch to an *-ing* word

- ❌ the production of
- ✅ producing

- ❌ the collection of
- ✅ collecting

- ❌ the reduction of
- ✅ reducing

- ❌ the elimination of
- ✅ eliminating

comment

Switch from an abstract noun to a stronger verb

- ✖ serves to make reductions
- ✔ reduces

- ✖ conduct an evaluation
- ✔ evaluate

- ✖ have a discussion
- ✔ discuss

- ✖ is an indication of
- ✔ indicates (or shows)

- ✖ give consideration to
- ✔ consider

- ✖ make a decision
- ✔ decide

- ✖ find a solution
- ✔ solve

- ✖ take an action
- ✔ act

Other common abstract nouns ending in *-ity* and *-ment* deserve similar treatment —changing *necessity* to *need,* and *commencement* to *start.*

links

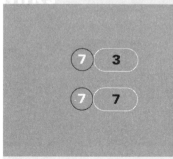

7 3

7 7

Words and phrases

Trim fat

Just as your
speech is filled
with words that
add nothing to
what you say,
your writing
often has words
that obscure
rather than
clarify your
meaning.

Trim such fat to
direct your
readers'
attention to
important words
and ideas.

Superfluous nouns

Superfluous nouns fatten many sentences and
distract attention from a stronger noun by relegating it to a prepositional phrase.

❌ **the field of** economics
✅ economics

Superfluous verbs

Idle, common verbs often supplant a working
verb, which becomes a noun: such verbs as *do,
have, is, make, provide,* and *serve.*

❌ **do** a study of the effects
✅ study the effects

Superfluous articles and prepositions

Articles and prepositions often prop up a noun
unnecessarily.

❌ **the** making **of** cloth
✅ making cloth

Overweight prepositions

Many overweight phrases needlessly detract
from the object they introduce by fattening a sentence.

❌ in regard to, in terms of, with respect to
✅ at, of, on, for, about

The opening *It*

Two classes of the opening *It* indicate fat. The first is *It is* . . . , *It was* . . . , or *It will be* . . . , followed by the subject, followed by *who, that,* or *which.*

❌ **It was** Wang Laboratories **that** engineered . . .
✅ Wang Laboratories engineered . . .

The second class is a series of circumlocutions —using many words where fewer will do—that begin with the indefinite pronoun *It.*

❌ **It appears that** Cuba will . . .
✅ Cuba will . . .

The opening *There*

Two classes of the opening *There* should be avoided. The first is the same as the first class of the opening *It.*

❌ **There are** some buildings **that** will . . .
✅ Some buildings will . . .

The second relegates what might precede the verb to less prominence after the verb.

❌ **There is** nothing wrong with . . .
✅ Nothing is wrong with . . .

In reviewing what you write, try to cut all unnecessary words and phrases—indeed, all unnecessary clauses, sentences, and paragraphs.

1	1
3	3
3	4
5	1
7	1
7	3

Words and phrases

Choose better words

technique	example

You should generally prefer words that are short, concrete, specific, and familiar.

Prefer short words to long

- ❌ accomplish
- ✅ do

- ❌ component
- ✅ part

- ❌ facilitate
- ✅ ease, help

- ❌ utilization
- ✅ use

Prefer concrete words to abstract

- ❌ motivation
- ✅ drive

- ❌ population
- ✅ people

Prefer specific words to general

- ❌ several
- ❌ a number of
- ✅ six

- ❌ vehicle
- ✅ car

comment

Prefer everyday language to jargon

- ✗ adult literacy rate
- ✓ percentage of people over fifteen who can read and write

- ✗ morbidity and mortality
- ✓ illness and death

If you must use jargon, define it in parentheses on its first appearance.

Prefer familiar words to unfamiliar

- ✗ nictitate
- ✓ wink

- ✗ defenestrate
- ✓ throw out of a window

- ✗ shrewdness of gorillas
- ✓ family of gorillas

Watch seeming synonyms

contemptible (deserving scorn)
contemptuous (scornful)

laudable (worthy of praise)
laudatory (expressing praise)

You can avoid many problems of word choice by keeping a dictionary within reach—and open.

Or by using an online dictionary (see the link below).

links

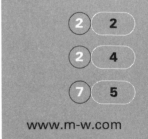

2 2

2 4

7 5

www.m-w.com

Words and phrases

Make pronoun references clear

**Few things slow
your readers
down more than
unclear pronoun
references—
signs of
carelessness
that quickly
distract them
from your
meaning.**

**Readers can
usually figure
out what you
mean. But why
make them go
to that effort?**

Ambiguous pronouns

If two or three nouns vie for a pronoun, the reference is almost certain to be ambiguous. The general solution is to repeat the noun rather than use a pronoun or to eliminate a competitor by changing its number.

✖ The main problem that **people** run into with **pronouns** is not tying **them** to nouns.

✔ The main problem that **people** run into with **pronouns** is not tying the **pronouns** to nouns.

✔ The main problem that **a writer** runs into with **pronouns** is not tying **them** to a noun.

Vague pronouns

If *this, that, these,* and *those* are used not as adjectives, as in *This book is* . . . , but as pronouns, as in *This is* . . . , they often are vague. If there is any question, however fleeting, about what the pronoun refers to, restore the noun or create one.

✖ The White House proposed an increase in aid to several Latin American countries. **This** has set off a barrage . . .

✔ The White House proposed an increase in aid to several Latin American countries. **This proposal** has set off a barrage . . .

Illogical pronouns

Some pronouns illogically stand for a noun that is implicit, not stated.

- ✗ Japan's exports of cars skyrocketed in the 1970s. The main reason is **their** skill in production.
- ✓ Japan's exports of cars skyrocketed in the 1970s. The main reason is the skill **of the Japanese** in production.

Other pronouns illogically stand for nouns of a different number: that is, a singular pronoun stands for a plural noun, a plural pronoun for a singular noun.

- ✗ **Everyone** has a right to the information **they** need to . . .
- ✓ **All people** have a right to the information **they** need to . . .
- ✓ **Everyone** has a right to the information **he or she** needs to . . .

Check each pronoun to be sure that there is no question about which noun the pronoun stands for.

5 3

Words and phrases

The elements of pairs and series usually appear as they come out of a writer's mind— haphazardly.

Rearranging those elements from short to long and from simple to compound makes the pair or series easier for readers to grasp.

Count the syllables

✖ ②letters and ①arts

✔ ①arts and ②letters

✖ ③oranges and ①pears

✔ ①pears and ③oranges

Count the words

✖ ②old-style politicians and ①reformers

✔ ①reformers and ②old-style politicians

✖ ⑤*Raiders of the Lost Ark,* ①*Shane,* and ④*Gone with the Wind*

✔ ①*Shane,* ④*Gone with the Wind,* and ⑤*Raiders of the Lost Ark*

✖ ③Nobility of spirit, ①modesty, and ②easy grace distinguished Bonhoeffer from his contemporaries.

✔ ①Modesty, ②easy grace, and ③nobility of spirit distinguished Bonhoeffer from his contemporaries.

comment

Put compound elements last

A compound element has more than one element, joined by *and*.

- ❌ He **washed the glasses, dishes, and silverware,** made the bed, **and** mopped the floor.
- ✅ He made the bed, mopped the floor, **and washed the dishes, glasses, and silverware.**

- ❌ **Salt and pepper,** tarragon, **and** mustard
- ✅ Mustard, tarragon, **and salt and pepper**

- ❌ **Red and yellow checks,** green stripes, **and** blue polka dots— all these were combined in an unpleasing farrago of patterns.
- ✅ Green stripes, blue polka dots, **and red and yellow checks**—all these were combined in an unpleasing farrago of patterns.

Exceptions

Obvious sequence or chronology: *breakfast, lunch, and dinner.*

Familiar or explicit order: *gold, frankincense, and myrrh.*

Alphabetical order: *Colombia, El Salvador, and Peru.*

links

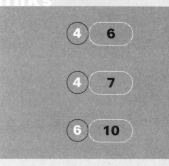

Keep pairs and trios parallel

Words and groups of words that do the same work are easier to read if they are similar (parallel) in grammatical construction.

One signal for words doing the same work is a single conjunction—an *and, but,* or *or*.

Another is a paired conjunction: *both . . . and; either . . . or; whether . . . or; not only . . . but also.*

Parallelism with single conjunctions

❌ the mama bear, the papa bear, **and their young cub**

✅ the mama bear, the papa bear, **and the baby bear**

❌ Do not fold, **put on a spindle, or mutilate.**

✅ Do not fold, **spindle, or mutilate.**

❌ He entered gingerly, **and she with recklessness.**

✅ He entered gingerly, **and she recklessly.**

❌ the good, the bad, **and ugly**

✅ the good, the bad, **and the ugly**

Parallelism with double conjunctions

❌ **Neither** a borrower **nor a person who borrows** money be.

✅ **Neither** a borrower **nor a lender** be.

❌ Revisionist historians suggest that FDR was **neither** a brilliant innovator **nor was he a man who believed** in abstractions.

✅ Revisionist historians suggest that FDR was **neither** a brilliant innovator **nor a believer** in abstractions.

comment

Elements are often not parallel because one of the pair is out of place.

- ✗ The sale of the land was opposed **both by** the environmentalists **and** the tourism lobby.
- ✔ The sale of the land was opposed **by both** the environmentalists **and** the tourism lobby.
- ✔ The sale of the land was opposed **both by** the environmentalists **and by** the tourism lobby.

- ✗ Solving the problem requires **that you both** recognize it **and that you** do something about it.
- ✔ Solving the problem requires **both that you** recognize it **and that you** do something about it.

Often the best solution is to go from a paired conjunction to a single.

- ✗ He has **not only** learned to draft reports **but also** to speak effectively.
- ✔ He has learned to draft reports **and** speak effectively.

- ✗ She went **both** to Italy **and** to France.
- ✔ She went to Italy **and** France.

The words and groups of words that follow each part of the pair should be parallel in construction.

links

4	6
4	7
6	10
7	1

Words and phrases

Shorten long sentences

Long sentences—those of more than, say, 20 to 25 words—are often hard to read. Short sentences usually are not.

Successions of long sentences are even harder to read—less so when broken up by the occasional short sentence.

Break a long sentence into two or more sentences

✖ The White House staff convinced the president that he should accept the transportation secretary's resignation and appoint a successor by noon on Friday, **and thus** press coverage soon focused not on policy issues but on the personality of the new secretary.

✔ The White House staff convinced the president that he should accept the transportation secretary's resignation and appoint a successor by noon on Friday. **Thus** press coverage soon focused not on policy issues but on the personality of the new secretary.

Cut unnecessary phrases and clauses

✖ The problem, **which remarkably few writers are aware of,** is that of failing to set off a non-restrictive clause by punctuation—**whether by commas, dashes, or parentheses.**

✔ The problem is that of failing to set off a nonrestrictive clause by punctuation.

Rearrange . . .

Even if the length of a sentence stays much the same, rearrangement and punctuation can give shape to otherwise amorphous elements.

 Striking a bit of terror in the hearts of all taxpayers, planting smiles on the faces of congressional staffers, and putting frowns on the faces of tax shelter buffs have been the three immediate effects of the IRS's draconian policies for assessing penalties.

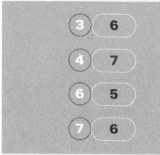 The IRS's draconian policies for assessing penalties have had three immediate effects: they have struck a bit of terror in the hearts of all taxpayers, planted smiles on the faces of congressional staffers, and put frowns on the faces of tax shelter buffs.

. . . and repunctuate

The judicious use of dashes can also set off parenthetical materials.

 At first glance, the elements of a painting, **which include line, form, light, color, subject, and representation,** are often overwhelmed by the total impression.

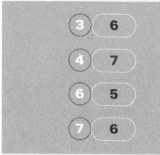 At first glance, the elements of a painting**—line, form, light, color, subject, and representation—** are often overwhelmed by the total impression.

The idea is not to be brief all of the time or even most of the time. The idea is to be brief unless you have a reason not to be.

3 6
4 7
6 5
7 6

Words and phrases

technique	example

If a *which* or *that* clause is defining the noun that it follows, use *that* with no punctuation.

If the clause is merely adding a comment about a noun that has already been defined or needs no definition, use *which* with punctuation.

Use *that* for clauses defining the noun

✖ The main problem **which most writers fail to deal with** is knowing the difference between defining and commenting clauses.

✔ The main problem **that most writers fail to deal with** is knowing the difference between defining and commenting clauses.

✖ The book **which he published last year** is on the forces of globalization.

✔ The book **that he published last year** is on the forces of globalization.

Punctuate clauses commenting on the noun

✖ His book on globalization **which he published last year** is about to be reprinted.

✔ His book on globalization, **which he published last year,** is about to be reprinted.

✔ His book on globalization, **published last year,** is about to be reprinted.

✖ The company **which is in its third round of takeover talks** has yet to turn a profit.

✔ The company, **which is in its third round of takeover talks,** has yet to turn a profit.

✔ The company, **in its third round of takeover talks,** has yet to turn a profit.

Note how you can often drop the *which is*.

Watch clauses that do not follow the noun they modify

Make the object of the prepositional phrase plural and rely on verb number

If this is still puzzling, you have plenty of company.

❌ The **meaning** of a **sentence,** which usually **is** obvious from . . .

✅ The **meaning** of **sentences,** which usually **is** obvious from . . .

Repeat the noun before the relative clause

✅ The meaning of a sentence, **meaning** that usually is obvious from . . .

Use the possessive form

✅ **A sentence's meaning,** which usually is obvious from . . .

Rewrite the sentence

✅ **The meaning of a sentence** *usually is obvious from* . . .

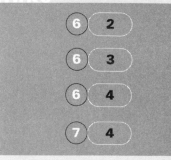

6　2

6　3

6　4

7　4

Words and phrases

Use the active voice

What's the difference between the active and passive voice?

If the subject acts, the voice is active. If the subject is acted on, the voice is passive.

The active voice is normally shorter, livelier, and more direct and so is usually preferred.

Identify the active and passive

(A) **The analysts reported** that the company would have earnings higher than they expected.

(P) **It was reported** that the company would have higher-than-expected earnings.

Switch from passive to active voice

Transpose the subject and the object.

✖ The bill **will have to be approved by** Congress.
✔ Congress **will have to approve** the bill.

✖ That book **was written by** Tom Wolfe.
✔ Tom Wolfe **wrote** that book.

Give the sentence an active subject.

✖ The book **was written** in 1994.
✔ **She wrote** the book in 1994.

✖ That the program is expected to be shut down.
✔ **Many people expect** that the administration will shut the program down.

✖ A new head **will be tapped** from the ranks.
✔ General Electric **will tap** a new head from its ranks.

When to use the passive voice

The passive voice has two justifiable uses, both turning on whether the actor is less important than what is acted on.

If the actor should be left out:

- ✖ **I manipulated** the variables to see whether I could determine the direction of causation.
- ✔ The variables **were manipulated** to determine the direction of causation.

If what is acted on is the subject of the paragraph:

- ✖ Jones, because of his experience in the Treasury, knows the budget. But **the president might soon ask him** to leave the Budget Office and take another position.
- ✔ Jones, because of his experience in the Treasury, knows the budget. But **he might soon be asked** by the president to leave the Budget Office and take another position.

Voice thus gives a choice. Too few writers take it, however, relying instead on the passive, which almost always takes more words.

7 2

7 3

Words and phrases

Be consistent

To be inconsistent is to be sloppy—say, by alternating between *traveled* and *travelled*, *10* and *ten*, or *%* and *percent*.

So try to be consistent—even if eccentric. The idea is to pick one style and stick to it.

A handy way to keep track of your choices for spelling, numbers, and the like is to store them on a style sheet.

Start with spelling choices and proceed to the others.

Spelling
Words with two or more acceptable spellings

- ✖ **judgment** on one page and **judgement** on the next
- ✔ **judgment** on one page and **judgment** on the next

Different words serving one function
- ✖ **Second** on one page and **secondly** on the next
- ✔ **Second** on one page and **second** on the next

Open, solid, and hyphenated terms
- ✖ **low-income** groups on one page and **low income** groups on the next
- ✔ **low-income** groups on one page and **low-income** groups on the next

Capitals
- ✖ the **project** on one page and the **Project** on the next
- ✔ the **project** on one page and the **project** on the next

Initials
- ✖ the **company retirement plan** on one page and the **CRP** on the next
- ✔ the **company retirement plan** on one page and the **company retirement plan** on the next

comment

Symbols and abbreviations

✖ **%** on one page and **percent** on the next
✔ **%** on one page and **%** on the next

✖ **television** on one page and **TV** on the next
✔ **television** on one page and **television** on the next

Numbers

✖ **0.5** on one page and **.5** on the next
✔ **0.5** on one page and **0.5** on the next

✖ **1994–95** on one page and **1994–1995** on the next
✔ **1994–95** on one page and **1994–95** on the next

Punctuation

✖ apples, oranges, **and** pears on one page and
apples, oranges **and** pears on the next
✔ apples, oranges, **and** pears on one page and
apples, oranges, **and** pears on the next

✖ **In 1990** the Russians . . . on one page and **In
1990,** the Russians . . . on the next
✔ **In 1990** the Russians . . . on one page and **In 1990**
the Russians . . . on the next

In most of the examples here it would have been acceptable (but not preferable) to have consistently chosen the second style.

Keep your style choices on a four-column document, which you can periodically print out for reference.

links

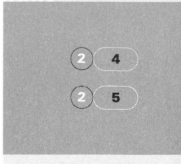

2 4

2 5

Credits

1. Light, layered, and linked

Lighten what you write
Benton Foundation, *Buildings, Books, and Bytes*. Washington, D.C., 1996,
  p. 37.

Link what you write
Sapient. [http://www.sapient.com/default htm].

2. Tools

Dictionaries and thesauruses
Babylon. [http://www.babylon.com].
Merriam-Webster. Database. [http://www.m-w.com].
OED (Operations Evaluations Department, World Bank). Database.
  [http://wbln0018.worldbank.org/oed/oedevent.nsf/htmlmedia/
  Interhome.html].

Format choices
Carl Dahlman and Jean-Eric Aubert, *China and the Knowledge Economy:
Seizing the 21st Century*. Washington, D.C.: World Bank, 2001, p. 1.

3. Attention-sustaining devices

Communicative contents
William Strunk Jr. and E. B. White, *The Elements of Style*. 2nd ed. New
York: Macmillan, 1972.
John Micklethwait and Adrian Wooldridge, "The Globalization Backlash,"
Foreign Policy, September–October 2001, pp. 16–26.
Peter Fingar, Ronald Aronica, Bryan Maizlish, *The Death of "e" and the Birth
of the Real New Economy: Business Models, Technologies & Strategies for
the 21st Century*. Tampa, Fla.: Meghan-Kiffer Press, 2001.

Credits

Light openings in print

"Special Report: Geography and the Net," *Economist,* August 11, 2001,
p. 18.

Christopher Conte, "Near Collisions Aloft Are Said to Be Rising as Air Traffic Picks Up," *Wall Street Journal,* April 20, 1984, p. A1.

David Brooks, "The Organization Kid," *Atlantic Monthly,* April 2001, p. 40.

Leila Jason, "Skipping Class 101," *Wall Street Journal,* August 22, 2001,
p. B1.

John Micklethwait and Adrian Wooldridge, "The Globalization Backlash,"
Foreign Policy, September–October 2001, p. 16.

Light openings on screen

Benton Foundation. Database. [http://www.benton.org/
Practice/Community/communitytips.html].

World Bank. Database. [http://www.worldbank.org/
knowledgebank/human.html].

Revealing headings

Amy Jo Kim, *Community Building on the Web: Secret Strategies for
Successful Online Communities.* Berkeley, Calif.: Peachpit Press, 2000,
pp. xiii–xiv.

Forum. "The 7 Deadly Sins of E-Learning." [http://www.forum.com/
magazine/feature-60.html]

Short paragraphs—and sentences

Toby Lester, "The Reinvention of Privacy," *Atlantic Monthly,* March 2001,
pp. 27–39, 28.

Carl Dahlman and Jean-Eric Aubert, *China and the Knowledge Economy:
Seizing the 21st Century.* Washington, D.C.: World Bank, 2001.

Bulleted lists

World Bank, *World Development Report 1998/1999*. Washington, D.C., 1999, p. 151.

Amy Jo Kim, *Community Building on the Web: Secret Strategies for Successful Online Communities*. Berkeley, Calif.: Peachpit Press, 2000, p. 205.

Amy Jo Kim, *Community Building on the Web: Secret Strategies for Successful Online Communities*. Berkeley, Calif.: Peachpit Press, 2000, p. 223.

Pull quotes

Leila Jason, "Skipping Class 101," *Wall Street Journal,* August 22, 2001, p. B1.

United Nations, *Human Development Report 2001*. New York: Oxford University Press, 2001, p. 30.

Mike Hofman, "Let's Get Physical," *Inc.*, special issue, *The Inc. 500,* October 17, 2000, p. 169.

James Fallows, "Freedom of the Skies," *Atlantic Monthly,* June 2001, p. 45.

Real quotes

Toby Lester, "The Reinvention of Privacy," *Atlantic Monthly,* March 2001, p. 27.

Toby Lester, "The Reinvention of Privacy," *Atlantic Monthly,* March 2001, p. 39.

Robert Kaplan, "Where Europe Vanishes," *Atlantic Monthly,* November 2000, p. 81.

Barbara Wallraff, "What Global Language?," *Atlantic Monthly,* November 2000, p. 58.

Boxes

United Nations, *Human Development Report 2001*. New York: Oxford University Press, 2001, p. 27.

Carl Dahlman and Jean-Eric Aubert, *China and the Knowledge Economy: Seizing the 21st Century*. Washington, D.C.: World Bank, 2001, p. 4.

Credits

Charts

Carl Dahlman and Jean-Eric Aubert, *China and the Knowledge Economy: Seizing the 21st Century.* Washington, D.C.: World Bank, 2001, p. 1.

TheStandard.com. [http://www.thestandard.com/article/0,1902,18909,00.html].

United Nations, *Human Development Report 2001.* New York: Oxford University Press, 2001, p. 33.

United Nations, *Human Development Report 2001.* New York: Oxford University Press, 2001, p. 108.

Tables

"Data Mine, The Launch," *Inc.,* special issue, *The Inc. 500,* October 17, 2000, p. 65.

Todd Davis, ed., *Open Doors: Report on International Educational Exchange, 1998–99.* New York: Institute of International Education, 1999, p. 15.

"Red Alert," *Economist,* July 21, 2001, p. 22.

"Ideal Employers," *Economist,* July 21, 2001, p. 56.

Diagrams

Bill Baker and Sophie Trémolet, "Micro Infrastructure: Regulators Must Take Small Operators Seriously," *Public Policy for the Private Sector,* September 2000, p. 21.

Bill Baker and Sophie Trémolet, "Access to Infrastructure: Let Competing Firms Offer a Mix of Price and Quality Options," *Public Policy for the Private Sector,* September 2000, p. 13.

Shirley O. Corriher, *Cookwise: The Hows and Whys of Successful Cooking.* New York: William Morrow, 1997, p. 40.

Shirley O. Corriher, *Cookwise: The Hows and Whys of Successful Cooking.* New York: William Morrow, 1997, p. 39.

Pictures

IBM. *IBM Annual Report 2000*. 2000, p. 16.

OECD (Organisation for Economic Co-operation and Development).
[http://www.peacecorps.gov].

4. Structures

Start with your main and supporting messages

U.S. Department of Commerce, *Warmer, Older, More Diverse: State by-
State Population Changes to 2025*. Washington, D.C., 1996.

Divide a subject into parts

U.S. Department of Commerce, *U.S. Industry and Trade Outlook 2000*.
New York: McGraw-Hill, 2000.

Arrange disparate details in logical groups

J. F. Rischard, *High Noon: 20 Global Issues, 20 Years to Solve Them*. New
York: Basic Books, 2002.

U.S. Department of Commerce, *Warmer, Older, More Diverse: State-by-
State Population Changes to 2025*. Washington, D.C., 1996.

Spell out a sequence

Scient. [http://www.scient.com/pc/about/eac/index.jsp].

Tell a story

David Crary, "Adoptees Battle Secrecy of Records," Associated Press, November 14, 2000.

Open a pyramid

Michael Waldholz, "Three-Drug Therapy May Suppress HIV," *Wall Street
Journal*, January 30, 1997.

Credits

Chronicle events
Anna Wilde Mathews, "Delayed Impact: Six Seconds, 2 Dead: A Police-Van Crash Exposes a Bombshell," *Wall Street Journal,* November 1, 1999.

Alternate between general and specific
Christopher Conte, "Will Workfare Work?," *Governing,* April 1996, pp. 19–23.

Create an outline of content-rich headings
Christopher Conte, *Fascinating Features.* Forthcoming.

Assemble a detailed plan
"The Best Strategies for Building Your Portfolio," *TIAA-CREF Participant,* August 2000.

5. Paragraphs

Keep them short
"The Failure of New Media," *Economist,* August 19–25, 2000, p. 53.
Nicholas Lehman, "The Battle over Boys," *New Yorker,* July 10, 2000, p. 79.
Lisa A. Choate and Dan E. Davidson, eds., *Cultural Handbook for the New Independent States.* Washington, D.C.: American Councils for International Education, p. 1.

Lead with the topic and point
Kenneth Hammonds, "Soul Proprietor," *Fast Company,* August 2000, p. 154.
Jeffrey Unger, "The Genuine Article?," *Fast Company,* October 2000, p. 392.
Chandler Burr, "Hollywood's New Game," *Fast Company,* December 2000, p. 253.
"V-Day for Vouchers?," *Economist,* July 15–21, 2000, p. 27.

Stick to one subject and verb form
"Unjammed," *Economist,* May 23–29, 1998, p. 74.

Ask a question and answer it
Sara Lawrence-Lightfoot, "Learning 101," *Fast Company,* October 2000, p. 134.

Douglas Preston, "The Temples of Angkor," *National Geographic,* August 2000, p. 90.

"Doubts, Hesitancy, Determination," *Economist,* February 14–20, 1998, p. 51.

"To Bury or to Praise," *Economist,* October 21–27, 1995, p. 27.

Repeat a key term
Alan Webber, "Steal These Ideas," *Fast Company,* August 2000, p. 16.

"Scribble, Scribble, Mr Gibbon," *Economist,* January 14–20, 1995, p. 75.

Max Frankel, "Goldilocks and the 3 Bulls," *New York Times Magazine,* January 5, 1997.

Repeat a sentence structure
"If Wall Street Falters," *Economist,* July 6–12, 1996, p. 19.

Alex Berenson, "No Longer Bulletproof, but Feeling Bullish Again," *New York Times,* July 23, 2000.

Kenneth Hammonds, "Soul Proprietor," *Fast Company,* August 2000, p. 164.

Count out the supporting sentences
Economist, April 27–May 3, 1991.

George Anders, "Pick Partnerships That Fit," *Fast Company,* October 2000, p.388.

"In Sickness and in Health," *Economist,* July 29–August 4, 2000, p. 20.

Credits

Use conjunctions

"The Trouble with Teams," *Economist,* January 14–20, 1995, p. 61.

"Blood Disorder," *Economist,* March 23–29, 1996, p. 49.

Claudia Deutsch, "When Top Jobs Go Begging," *New York Times,* November 1, 2000.

Use other signals

"Goodwill—and a Group of Islands," *Economist,* October 24–30, 1998.

Use bullets

United Nations Development Programme, *Human Development Report 2001: Making New Technologies Work for Development.* New York: Oxford University Press, 2001, p. 19.

Bill Breen, "Where Are You on the Map?," *Fast Company,* January 2001, p. 108.

Link your paragraphs

Ron Lieber, "Boing!," *Fast Company,* November 2000, p. 348.

"Who Speaks for Cyberspace?," *Economist,* January 14–20, 1995, p. 64.

6. Sentences

Leading parts

Alessandra Stanley, "From Perestroika to Pizza: Gorbachev Stars in TV Ad," *New York Times,* December 3, 1997.

"The Death of Distance," in *A Survey of Telecommunications* (insert), *Economist,* September 30–October 6, 1995, p. 5.

"Work in Progress," *Economist,* July 26–August 1, 1999, p. 21.

"Banking Laws," *Economist,* July 26–August 1, 1999, p. 69.

Inner parts

World Bank, *World Development Report 1999/2000*. New York: Oxford University Press, 2000, p. 107.

Unattributed, "Easter Island's Lures: Statues and Rock Art," *New York Times,* October 29, 2000.

Daniel Costello and Bob Hughes, "Arts and Culture Abroad," *Wall Street Journal,* June 25, 1999.

Kirk Johnson, "Return of the Natives: Playing God in the Fields," *New York Times,* November 12, 2000.

Trailing parts

Mary Lee Settle, *Turkish Reflections: A Biography of a Place.* New York: Simon & Schuster, 1992, p. 26.

Neela Banerjee, "Can Black Gold Ever Flow Green?," *New York Times,* November 12, 2000.

Mary Tabor, "Big Advance? No, Thanks, He'll Publish It Himself," *New York Times,* September 24, 2000.

"Michel von Clemm," *Economist,* December 22–28, 1997, p. 105.

Economist October 7, 1995, p. 23.

Occasional short forms

World Bank, *World Development Report 1998/99.* New York: Oxford University Press, 1999, p. 17.

United Nations Development Programme, *Human Development Report 2000.* New York: Oxford University Press, 2000, p. 34.

"Preparing America for Compassionate Conservatism," *Economist,* July 29–August 4, 2000, p. 23.

Credits

Dramatic flourishes

"Politics This Week," *Economist*, July 15–21, 2000, p. 6.

Alan Webber, "Steal These Ideas," *Fast Company*, August 2000, p. 16.

Bruce Mau, "Design Principal," *Fast Company*, October 2000, pp. 178–79.

Robert Joss, "Robert Joss," *Fast Company*, August 2000, p. 90.

Henry R. Luce, *The American Century*. New York: Farrar and Rinehart, 1941, p. 33.

Elegant repetitions

"Where Worlds Collide," *Economist*, August 19–25, 2000, p. 17.

"System Failure," in International Banking Survey, *Economist*, April 27–May 3, 1996, p. 6.

Credible quotations

Michiko Kakutani, "The United States of Andy," *New York Times Magazine*, November 17, 1996.

"We Know You're Reading This," *Economist*, February 10–16, 1996, p. 27.

The Benton Foundation, *What's Going On*. Washington, D.C.: Benton Foundation, 1997, p. 10.

Rick Lyman, "Mae Questel, 89, Behind Betty Boop and Olive Oyl," *New York Times*, January 8, 1998.

Robert Hughes, "American Visions," *Time*, May 21, 1997, p. 37.

Meg Greenfield, "Unsexing the Military," *Newsweek*, June 16, 1997, p. 80.

Roxanne Roberts, "Holiday Park's Senior Class," *Washington Post*, June 2, 1997.

Coversational injections

Andrew Delbanco, "The Great Leviathan," *New York Review of Books,* May 15, 1997, p. 18.

Robert J. Samuelson, "Telephone Staddle," *Washington Post,* May 14, 1997, p. 21.

"Where Worlds Collide," *Economist,* August 19–25, 2000, p. 17.

"A Turning Point for AIDS?," *Economist,* July 15–21, 2000, p. 78.

Michiko Kakutani, "To Hell with Him," *New York Times Magazine,* December 7, 1997, p. 37.

Deft connections

Ian Fisher, "The No-Complaints Generation," *New York Times Magazine,* October 5, 1997, p. 68.

Seth Schiesel, "Web Hardware Maker Buys Digital 'Plumber' for $41 Billion," *New York Times,* July 11, 2000.

T. Coraghessan Boyle, "Friendly Skies," *New Yorker,* August 7, 2000, p. 71.

"The Failure of New Media," *Economist,* August 19–25, 2000, p. 55.

Tracy Kidder, "The Good Doctor," *New Yorker,* July 10, 2000, p. 51.

"The End of the Affair," *Economist,* August 19–25, 2000, p. 28.

Richard W. Stevenson, "Anticipate Financial Crises and Prepare, Greenspan Says," *New York Times,* July 13, 2000.

Kenneth Hammonds, "Soul Proprietor," *Fast Company,* August 2000, p. 162.

Credits

One-syllable openings

Tom Peters, "You Say You Want a Revolution," *Fast Company,* October 2000, p. 94.

Ronald White, "Giving Back 01," *Fast Company,* December 2000, p. 136.

Bryan DiSalvatore, "Postcard from Missoula," *New Yorker,* September 25, 2000, p. 34.

William Safire, "Day of Infamy," *New York Times Magazine,* December 7, 1997, p. 30.

"Panic in South Korea," *Economist,* December 13–19, 1997, p. 16.

Gretchen Morgenson, "Bond Believers See Prelude to a Fall," *New York Times,* November 19, 2000.

"Drop That Steak or We Shoot," *Economist,* December 13–19, 1997, p. 15.

"All This, and a Korean Election Too," *Economist,* December 13–19, 1997, p. 34.

David Handelman, "The Ambivalent-about-Prime-Time-Players," *New York Times Magazine,* December 28, 1997, p. 28.

7. Words and phrases

Search for *and*

"The Death of Distance," in *A Survey of Telecommunications* (insert), *Economist,* September 20–October 6, 1995, p. 5.

"Musical Moments," *Economist,* July 24–30, 1999, p. 80.

Search for *which*

William Strunk Jr. and E. B. White, *The Elements of Style.* 2nd ed. New York: Macmillan, 1972.

Index

Index

ClearWriter

"It's like having a writing instructor and an editor in your PC"

Bruce Ross-Larson, author of *Writing for the Information Age,* is also the author of the *Effective Writing Series.* Whether you're composing a Web page, crafting an interoffice memo, or agonizing over an annual budget report, the *Effective Writing Series* is the key to clarity, accuracy, and economy in any writing task. And the techniques introduced in the series are now available online as ClearWriter™.

ClearWriter is the next-generation complete training solution for effective business and professional writing. ClearWriter contains 25 courses in a library with four broad subject areas: editing your own writing, improving your sentence structures, building more powerful paragraphs, and writing more effective reports. The 15 hours of online training are highly interactive and provide context-based feedback.

Rating:
★★★★★

Award Winning Course:

LGUIDE
EDITOR'S
CHOICE
AWARD
FALL 2001

Publisher:

ClearWriter received Lguide's prestigious Editor's Choice Award!!

ClearEdits® is a Microsoft® Word plug-in that applies the many editing techniques from *Edit Yourself*, part of the *Effective Writing Series.* ClearEdits suggests improvements in clarity and readability in a fraction of the time it takes to edit a document unassisted. And it can be customized to catch the problems that plague an individual's writing most—for maximum impact and improvement.

ClearEdits

Learn more online at www.clearwriter.com
Save 10% on ClearWriter or ClearEdits with promotional code IA110

AUG 2 6 2002